Please accept this book as a comp[...] [...] to the [...] nuances of golf and getting started [...] [...] golf. My gratitude to Debbie Waitkus for her dedication to the game of golf. Her genuine love of golf and those who play it, is evidenced by her writing this book.

I would like to thank you for entrusting me with your golf journey as your golf coach. You will learn a lot about yourself and others, as the game of golf mirrors life in so many ways.

Be mindful of these three **FUN**damentals as you play golf:

FAST-Keep up with the group in front of you at all times, even if you have to pick up your ball and move on to the next hole to get caught up.

SAFE-Do not endanger others with your golf club or ball. Be aware of your surrounding at all times.

COURTEOUS-Be nice to the environment and those within the environment. Use the "Golden Rule".

Lastly, a heartfelt thank you to my Dad, Matt Gunby, who taught me how to play golf, was my mentor and will always be my hero. To me, he was the greatest man that ever walked the earth except for Jesus. He taught me that the only reason we are here is help one another. He allowed me to face and fight through many challenges. Along with his passion for golf, his love and integrity will be with me forever. I love you Dad!

Keep Golf Great!
John Gunby, PGA
gunnergolf@hotmail.com
602-628-4243

"*Get Your Golf On!* is a wonderful handbook to accompany your golf instruction and get you playing the game. Ultimately, you have to feel like you belong in the sport. This little book will have you feeling like a golfer before you ever take the first swing.

"Debbie Waitkus covers the basics in what to wear, what equipment you need, and how to navigate around the course. She introduces you to 'golf lingo' and speaks to you as a supportive friend, sharing stories and quotes from others that have ventured into this game. Their insight will give you the confidence to accept invitations to play, and inspire you to ask others to play with you. So, take your lessons from an LPGA or PGA Professional, read this handbook and join us at the course. We are waiting for you on the tee!"

~ *Sandy LaBauve, LPGA and PGA Class A Teaching Professional,*
Founder of LPGA*USGA Girls Golf

"Debbie's book is a WINNER! This all-inclusive golf book covers everything a new golfer wants and needs to know on the journey from the initial understanding of equipment, apparel, terminology, rules, and etiquette to the importance of skill development, and finally, taking those skills to the golf course to play this wonderful game we all love... a terrific progression that will help the knowledge, transfer, and comfort level of every new golfer. I recommend this book to my students as it effectively answers so many of the questions new players tend to have in a friendly and easy to understand manner. The stories that are shared throughout the book show the significant connection between business and golf... a very nice addition. Congratulations, Debbie... well done!"

~ *Deb Vangellow, LPGA Master Professional, LPGA Past National President,*
Riverbend Country Club - Houston, Texas

"In this wonderful little book are the keys for easy access to my happy place— and it can become yours too—the golf course! *Get Your Golf On!* is a delightful collection of tips, anecdotes, information, and expertise collected from people who love the game and wish to share it with you."

~ *Nancy Lopez, LPGA, World Golf Hall of Fame*

"In this easy to read guide for beginning golfers, Debbie Waitkus of Golf for Cause shares her enthusiasm for the game and encouragement for all those women who want to play golf but are perhaps too intimidated to start. Beginning with her own story of hitting the course for the first time, she answers every question a beginning golfer is likely to ask. What to wear, what equipment to buy, borrow or rent, where to practice, and basic tips about golf etiquette and rules every golfer should know. Including reflections from a wide variety of recreational and professional golfers, *Get Your Golf On!* offers inspiration for every beginning golfer. Deb's goal in writing the book was to remove the fear factor so many new golfers face. *Get Your Golf On!* does just that."

~ *Pat Mullaly, Editor, GolfGurls.com*

"Any female who is toying with the idea of playing golf but is nervous about what to expect will love this book. It breaks down the fear-factor and anxiety so many novice female golfers have about playing golf, especially since it's such a male dominated sport and there are very few resources for us women. Even as an avid golfer, I found it interesting and really fun to read.

"What I really enjoyed is how descriptive Debbie is in explaining the various aspects of the game from what equipment to use, how it's used to what gear you need and why. Even what to do at the range. *Get Your Golf On!* answers every question a new golfer has about playing golf. The dialogue made me feel like I was having a one-on-one chat with one of my best friends about golf. Brilliant!"

~ *Christina Thompson, Founder & CEO Golf4Her*

"A valuable book for so many types of golfers: tentative 'not sure if I want to get into this game' golfers, those just starting out or even playing for a couple of years, and experienced golfers looking to improve their personal or business relationships through golf. I highly recommend this to golfers of all skill levels and will encourage my students to get a copy today! A fabulous guide for building your confidence in the game of golf."

~ *Char Carson, LPGA Teaching Professional*

"What an impressive collection of universal experiences! Rich with information and common-sense advice, this book is the next best thing to having a personal golf mentor. Throughout the book are reflections of women who became Debbie's (the author's) friends. They are women who enjoy golf and its social, business and health advantages. Their anecdotes relate what can happen to you when you *Get Your Golf On!*"

~ *Jan Bel Jan, ASGCA Golf Course Architect, Jan Bel Jan*
Golf Course Design, 2019-2020 President ASGCA

"Here's a book that makes a perfect gift for the woman you'd like to play golf with, except that she doesn't play. For all of the advancements in golf for women, the game still puts off newbies. The guys will just bluff their way through the awkwardness of picking up a new sport, but women want to feel welcome, invited, competent. With *Get Your Golf On!* Debbie Waitkus has succeeded in presenting a smart, friendly invitation to women by giving them all the information they need to feel comfortable at a golf course.

"She's not teaching the swing, the chip and the putt; rather, she offers tips on learning and practicing, plus all of the ancillary information required to make a tee time, check in, dress appropriately, keep score, navigate the golf course and observe all of the important etiquette and important rules."

~ *Susan Fornoff, Gotta Go Golf*

"*Get Your Golf On!* is an easy read with specific tools to build your golf confidence and knowledge of what this fabulous game is all about. It will definitely give you knowledge to get you on the "radar screen" of your colleagues and bosses. As women, we want to know as much as possible about what we are getting into. So, for those of you looking to get into the sport of golf, *Get Your Golf On!* will certainly help you with your learning curve. It's a 'high five read."

~ *Pam Swensen, P.S. Let's Talk Golf*

"*Get Your Golf On!* is a must read and a fun read for all entering this great game of golf. The reader will surely enjoy the stories from all who took that first step to start the game and finally taking the big first step on the first tee. Play On!"

~ *Lynn Stellman, LPGA Class A Member, LPGA T&CP Hall of Fame,*
LPGA & Golf Digest Best Women Teachers In The USA

"As a relatively new golfer I was fortunate to have as my first mentor a women business professional. Not only did she teach me to play from the forward tees in the beginning ("you'll learn faster" is all I needed to hear), but she helped school me in the art and science of building relationships on the golf course. Women are natural relationship builders, and since then I've learned that they therefore have a huge advantage in playing business golf with men. I strongly encourage you share this book with anyone you know that wants to have more prosperity, energy and joy, it's a book I wish I had when I started to learn to play golf ten years ago."

~ *Tom Matzen, International best-selling author, speaker and serial entrepreneur @ravingfans4life*

"Debbie is a friend who has worked tirelessly to empower women through the game of golf. As a PGA Professional and LPGA T & CP Professional, we welcome all women to get out on the golf course to enjoy everything golf has to offer. As Debbie's title states, read this book and *Get Your Golf On!*"

~ *Suzy Whaley, Director of Instruction Suzy Whaley Golf, Golf Digest Top 50 Instructor, 2019 President, PGA of America*

"If you are new to golf, or thinking about becoming new to golf, this is the book for you. Deb covers everything you need to know or may want to know about how to find your own joy in the game and find success in all that surrounds golf. You will probably find yourself keeping this as a reference to refer to as you progress in the game"

~ *Larry Berle, Author, A Golfer's Dream, www.GolfersDreamBook.com*

"*Get Your Golf On!* answers the questions aspiring golfers don't want or don't know to ask, and shares core information to prepare them for their first round. With its humor and inspiring anecdotes, it is a must read for the beginning golfer."

~ *Elizabeth Noblitt, Integrity Styling*

"At the intersection of passion and interest with a dose of insight and practical suggestions is Deb Waitkus' new guide for those who want to take the game of golf up and are just not quite sure what questions to answer let alone ask. Her long involvement with the game as a passionate advocate for all of the good that it plays in our lives is very much evident in the great anecdotes she collected and the very helpful, easy to understand guide tips she provides to get you over the threshold. I have already read it once and even with my familiarity with the game picked up a few new tips and know with my second reading I will pick up a few more. *Get Your Golf On!* has me moving to the first tee."

~ *Donna Orender, Orender Unlimited, LLC*

"This book is awesome. Perfect for newcomers to the game as well as a terrific refresher for veterans. Great job Debbie!"

~ *Linda Dillenbeck, The Image Group*

"Be inspired by *Get Your Golf On!* It's a must read for all golfers! Debbie brilliantly weaves anecdotes of a journey into the game of golf resulting in an informative and entertaining read!

~ *Debbie O'Connell, President Live Positive and Golf Positive, Class A LPGA Teaching Professional*

"I've had the pleasure of both playing golf with Deb and, being in an environment where her expertise in the area of golf, business golf and her keen understanding of 'human nature' were able to shine through. Deb's insights into all things golf from the perspective of women playing with men and men playing with women is truly unsurpassed. She has it figured out!

"Through *Get Your Golf On!* she brings a thoughtful practicality to the game that considers not only the rules of the game but the frailness of us as people in a setting where anxiety can easily rule the day. Deb makes it fun, relaxed and yet purposeful. Her understanding of the nuances of this wonderful yet at times, frustrating pastime make her book a must read for anyone just starting out with the game or as a great reminder for those of us who are more seasoned.

"If you play golf for business or pleasure, *Get Your Golf On!* is the perfect book for your bedside."

~ *Allen Bonk, President & CEO – Rinno Technologies, Inc.*

"Golf can be complicated. There are so many equipment options, rules of play and etiquette lessons designed to keep the game honorable. *Get Your Golf On!* educates the reader on all these subjects and more in an easy-to-follow format. It's a fun read with realistic examples that set up the reader for success both on and off the course."

~ *Jill Strite, Founder Versatile Golf, LPGA Teaching Professional*

"*Get Your Golf On!* is excellent! I am very pleased by your insight on the many unknowns a beginner has about starting in golf. It is a must read for every woman, (and male too), who is picking up the game. It answers a lot of questions with very useful and quite accurate information of the ins and outs of golf as it is played in the 21st century."

~ *Peter Longo, "The King Of Clubs," Former PGA Tour Player, Trick Shot Champion*

"From the front cover with a picture of gals just having fun, to the back cover with author Debbie Waitkus and LPGA Co-founder Marilynn Smith, *Get Your Golf On!* is a must-have resource for new golfers, and a wonderful reference for more seasoned players.

"*Get Your Golf On!* puts FUN into the FUNdamentals of golf. I love the lessons contained in the anecdotes that complement every chapter - all add extra value and meaning for the female golfer wanting to become engaged in the game.

"I am very impressed with this book and share it with our Golf Fore Gals members and guests whenever I can. Thanks, Debbie for a fantastic resource for us female golfers, and for your energy and wisdom that is apparent throughout the book.

~ *Diane Fru, Owner, Golf Fore Gals, British Columbia and Maui*

"I'm not going to lie, when I first bought this book, I thought it would be another dry 'how to play the game' book. But to my surprise, *Get Your Golf On!* is the best beginners guide to golf on the market for women. If you are a woman thinking about getting into golf or are a man who knows of a woman thinking about getting into golf this is the book to read! Debbie's style is as flowing as a Harry Potter novel but is packed full of great tips and etiquette that will make you feel comfortable on the course. Forget keeping a rule book in your bag. Debbie Waitkus' book *Get Your Golf On!* is the new rule book for the casual female golfer!"

~ *Jenn Harris, CEO, High Heel Golfer*

Get Your GOLF On!

Your Guide to Getting in the Game

2nd Edition

by Debbie Waitkus

GOLF FOR CAUSE

Get Your Golf On!
2nd Edition

Photography by Jim Amrine

Cover design and interior layout by Brandi Hollister, Mullins Creative
www.mullinscreative.com

Published by
Golf for Cause®, LLC
1050 N. 52nd St., Phoenix, AZ 85008
www.golfforcause.com

ISBN # 978-0-9858220-2-6

Acknowledgements

Get Your Golf On! started as an idea. An idea that I placed on a tee and, like some things in life, it stayed on that tee until I finally stepped up and took a swing, sending it into play. With much joy and appreciation, that idea is now in your hands! I had a lot of encouragement and support along the way… from tee to green.

Joining me on the tee, I'm thankful to all the Nine & Winers — with special thanks to the amazing mentors, particularly Char Carson, whose passion and commitment to growing others through golf always shines, along with Kevin and Cindy Sonoda.

Laura Martini, thanks for inviting me to play and insisting that we'd have fun and I'd just love it! Who knew?! And to Bower Yousse, Maurine Karabatsos, Silver Rose and Joyce (Rosie) Friel, thank you for your strong presence on the tee!

Advancing *Get Your Golf On!* down the fairway, thank-you Jake Poiner for helping me keep my ball in play! High fives to some of the best playing partners around: Jan Bel Jan with Jan Bel Jan Golf Course Design; Le Ann Finger, PGA, LPGA with the Arizona Golf Association; Pam Wright, LPGA; Kathy Murphy, LPGA; Karen Gleason with Glove It; Taba Dale with The Scottsdale Collection; Peggy Gustafson, LPGA; Sue Wieger, LPGA; Jill Strite, LPGA; Portland Reed; my colleagues in Women in the Golf Industry (WIGI) — special shout outs to Kathy Bissell with Coldwell Banker; Emmy Moore Minister with Moore Minister Consulting Group; Christina Thompson with Golf4Her; Christina Ricci, LPGA; Sandi LaBauve with LaBauve Golf Academy and Barbara Gutstadt with Women's Golf & Travel. And to the TTFNers, way to keep golf (and life) fun — always! Larry Wilk needs special mention for teaching me the finer points of golf — like matching beverage selections to my wardrobe, and Lana Hock for the importance of a great golf wardrobe… especially the hats!

Marilynn Smith, I miss you terribly! I loved your trailblazing spirit, can-do attitude and voice in my head reminding me to "hold my finish" — a great reminder to step up to the tee and to follow through on everything I do. Shirley Spork, I promise to hold all my quarters and dimes!

Thanks to my children who know that golf is fun! Ben — always ready with a bet for shots over the water. Amy, who dribbled the ball off the tee at her first Nine & Wine outing and decided that she'd just ride in the cart for the day, was inspired to play and proclaimed golf as being "fun" after she watched one of her playing partners tee up a ball in the fairway for her second shot.

Clearly my favorite playing partners in the entire world are my husband, Jack Waitkus, the Ireland Crew ♪ and my mom Lois (who learned to play golf in her 60s when she married Maury, a passionate four-time-a-week golfer — thanks, Maury!). She read the manuscript and proclaimed it the Bible! Without their help *Get Your Golf On!* would never have made it to the green.

Vickie Mullins with Perfect Bound Marketing, thank you for tending the flag on my final hole, helping me sink the putt! Hats off to photographer extraordinaire, Jim Amrine, now, the newest golfer to be seen at the driving range — despite the Arizona summer heat and his two artificial hips!

You'll read what I hope you'll find to be inspirational quotes and words of golf wisdom throughout *Get Your Golf On!* from friends who were willing to share their insights about golf with you. (Golf is a great way to collect friends!) Many thanks to Mary Alexander, Jessica Boutwell, Helen Burland, Char Carson, Margaret Dunn, Le Ann Finger, Jason Glashan, Yvette Gonzales, Gail Grace, Zoe Gryparis, Jim Hall, Edythe Higgins, Debbie Hill, Lana Hock, Maurine Karabatsos, Sandy LaBauve, Ann Lieff, Nancy Lopez, Stephanie McCoy Loquvam, Jean Ann Morris, Gayle Moss, Debbie O'Connell, Kate Rakoci, Portland Reed, Shirley Spork, Robin Stowell, Jill Strite, Rich Strozewski, Allison Suriano, Christina Thompson, Amy Waitkus and Pam Wright.

And to my caddie — Bower Yousse, my permanent guest at the 19th hole, I appreciate you carrying my bag and helping me find my voice. Without your collaboration, *Get Your Golf On!* would still be sitting on the tee.

Table of Contents

Foreword

At ages 10, 11 and 12, I was the pitcher, coach and manager of a boys' baseball team in my hometown of Wichita, Kansas — and thought nothing of being the only one sporting pigtails under my cap. My sights were set on being a pitcher for the St. Louis Cardinals baseball team.

One day I came home after pitching a game and my mom asked, "How did you do today, dear?" I threw my glove across the room and said a few choice words that I had learned from the boys. My mother marched me to the lavatory and washed out my mouth with Lifebuoy soap.

When my dad arrived home and learned what I had said, he responded with something that would change my life: "We'd better take her out to the Wichita Country Club and teach her a more ladylike sport." Interestingly, girls in the 1940s weren't supposed to play sports, let alone golf — we were supposed to get married and raise families.

That also rang true when I went to the University of Kansas, which didn't have a golf team for girls at the time. Moreover, when my dad asked the University's athletic director, Phog Allen, if there might be some expense money so I could play in the National Intercollegiate Championship at the Ohio State Golf Course, he responded, "Mr. Smith, it's too bad your daughter is not a boy."

 Looking back, despite some bumps along the way, things turned out better than a freckled, pigtailed girl from Kansas ever could have hoped. Golf gave me an opportunity to excel at a sport and therefore to pursue a dream. I've always felt that God put me in the right place at the right time. A baker's dozen of us founded the LPGA in 1950, drumming up support for the tour as well as playing on it. I cherish every tournament memory with my friends — the 21 victories, two major championships, and induction into the World Golf Hall of Fame were simply delicious icing on an incredible cake.

Thanks to golf, I've had the opportunity to make friends in all 50 states and in 37 countries around the world, broadening my horizons in ways that I have to pinch myself to believe. I've performed exhibitions at air bases in France and Germany, and I've been fortunate enough to meet six U.S. Presidents. And, for more than a decade, golf has enabled me to pay it forward with charity tournaments to support the Marilynn Smith Scholarship Fund, which helps young women go to college.

Golf is a humbling game, and it teaches you something new every time you step up to the tee. It reveals your own character — and the character of those around you. But, more than anything, it underscores the amazing things that happen when you enjoy what you're doing and grow with the results.

That, for me, is at the heart of this book. I met Debbie Waitkus when she played in the Marilynn Smith LPGA Charity Pro Am in 2009. Unbeknownst to me, she was in the audience at my induction ceremony into the World Golf Hall of Fame and subsequently wrote a story about me, which was published. We became fast friends, and her efforts, energy and talent as the co-tournament director of the Pro Am have made it possible for hundreds of college-bound ladies to earn scholarships. She's a jewel.

I think you'll find that Debbie's approach to introducing new golfers to this wonderful game is a drive straight down the middle.

Marilynn Smith *(1929 – 2019)*
LPGA Co-Founder; LPGA President (1958 – 1960)
World Golf Hall of Fame Inductee (2006)
Winner of 21 LPGA tournaments including 2 majors
Inaugural Patty Berg Award Recipient (1978)
Created and promoted the first Senior LPGA tournament (2001)
Started LPGA TC&P (Teaching & Club Professional) Division
*   with Shirley Spork (1959)*
Conducted over 4,000 golf clinics
Member of 11 Halls of Fame

Prelude to Your Adventure...

Pam Wright

Anyone who plays golf understands how challenging it can be. But, as a result of the game's challenges, players gain an inherent respect for each other — particularly those who play the game as it was intended. By joining the game, you are also joining an extended social family with its own set of rules and traditions, and a cast of fun, interesting and entertaining characters.

As a reader of this book, you're undoubtedly coming to the sport from a bit of a different angle than my own. My dad was a golf pro in my native Scotland, and my mom played at a very high level in her own right. I first picked up a club at age four, earned a college scholarship to Arizona State University, and enjoyed a 15-year playing career on the LPGA Tour.

In the years since retiring from the LPGA Tour, I've had the good fortune to stay in the game as a golf instructor and coach, my true passion! About a third of my students are new golfers, though the overall talent pool runs the gamut — and, truth be told, playing golf for 30 years doesn't mean you will break 100. Thankfully golf is about so much more than keeping score.

I've found that, for many new to the game, the biggest hurdle is the process of becoming comfortable — or, as many of my students have expressed it, overcoming the anxiety of "I don't know if I can do that" or "what am I supposed to do here?" That's exactly what Debbie's book is all about — preparing to experience the game, no matter your style, just being yourself doing so.

I believe a new golfer's greatest asset is often enthusiasm. It's always insipiring to have someone on the lesson tee who's "into it," regardless of the specific motivation for learning to play. When that person heads out on the course, it can even rekindle the spark for more experienced and serious players who have long ago forgotten the thrill of their first good shots. They just have to stop and say, "Wow, she's having a blast!"

As an adult beginner, after all, you're in a unique position — you're starting out as someone who's *choosing* to venture out onto the tees, fairways and greens. My best advice is to surround yourself with people who make it enjoyable. Go with some friends, hit some shots, get some help from an instructor and and, most importantly, enjoy yourself.

Golf's a game. Keep it fun!
Pam Wright
Pam Wright Golf
www.pamwrightgolf.com

1989 LPGA Rookie of the Year
1990, 1992, 1994 Solheim Cup Competitor
2000, 2002 Solheim Cup Vice Captain
22 Top 10 finishes on LPGA Tour
Recorded lowest 9-hole score of 30 in US Open history
Arizona State University Hall of Fame
Two-time Pac-10 Champion
Academic All-American
Two Time All-American
1979 – 1987 Scottish Internationalist

Introduction

When I was pregnant, I had on my nightstand a copy of *What to Expect When You're Expecting.*

It was a popular book with moms-to-be because it prepared you for what was to come and provided reassurance you'd survive the experience just fine. I soon learned no book can prepare a person 100% for delivery day and diapers, but I found it helpful in understanding the scope of what I'd gotten myself into. It is the memory of that book that inspired this book.

I can report that nine months of pregnancy and taking up the game of golf aren't that much alike, but over the years I've encountered many newcomers who arrive at *Golf for Cause* clinics and outings with delivery-room anxiety. The majority of them are women.

I admit that setting out to become a golfer can be an intimidating experience, especially if you don't have a clue where to begin. It is, for almost everyone. It was for me.

My goal for *Get Your Golf On!* is to remove the intimidation factor so that starting out can be easy for you and playing will always be fun. This isn't an instruction book on how to hit a golf ball, however. You learn to do *that* by hitting golf balls and taking lessons, although taking lessons is not mandatory (Bubba Watson, 2012 and 2014 Masters Champion, has never had a lesson). Nonetheless, your local teaching professional can help you advance your game.

Get Your Golf On! draws on my experience and the experiences of thousands of new golfers who have participated in *Golf for Cause*

Nine & Wine golf mentoring outings. *Nine & Wine* participants have fun learning to look, act, think, talk and laugh the way golfers do. They even play nine holes! The objective is to demystify golf so completely for participants that, when they leave, they can go to any golf course and feel confident and comfortable.

So, get your golf on and begin the wonderful experience that will enrich your life in countless ways.

~ Debbie Waitkus

Living a Dream

"It took me 45 years to discover my love for golf, but once I experienced the joys of playing the game and challenging myself to get better, I've never looked back. For me, golf is much more than "a game for life;" golf IS my life.

"My father and brother were avid golfers, but in my youth, boys golfed and girls figure skated. When I moved to Vancouver, BC in 2003 I saw that people enjoyed golf here year round — a rare thing in Canada. I was dating a man at the time who hadn't played golf in years but wanted to take it up again. So after decades of playing spectator, I decided to give it a try in 2004.

"After some excellent instruction and a few "come back tomorrow" shots, I've become addicted to all things golf and started writing about it — first on my golfgal.ca blog, then on *Golf for Women Magazine's* website and now for InsideGolf.ca. When I'm not playing golf or writing about it, I am an independent marketing consultant. I am often asked by clients to play golf with them and their customers, which helps grow my network and business opportunities.

"On the personal side, I am now married to that man who encouraged me to take up the sport in 2004. He loves the game almost as much as I do and is my first choice in a playing partner. Golf gave us a dream and we're living it!"

Gayle Moss
Marketing Consultant
www.on-mark-it.com

Little Did I Know

"Don't fear failure so much that you refuse to try new things. The saddest summary of a life contains three descriptions: could have, might have, and should have."

~ *Louis E. Boone*

When you are learning something new, it's important to trust the person teaching you. You have to believe your teacher has credibility that she knows what she is talking about. To establish my street, or "grass" cred, here is the story of my first golf experience. (If you think *you* don't know enough about golf, listen to this!)

I didn't discover golf on my own. I discovered golf only after a friend dragged me into it.

Laura was a colleague whose uncle had recently begun teaching her to play. Almost overnight she had become an enthusiast, a fanatic actually, and she was determined to get me involved too. "Come on, Debbie," she pleaded. "Just give it a try. I know you'll love it!"

I knew I wouldn't love it. I'd grown up playing every sport a girl could play, except golf. Golf didn't interest me. It sounded boring. But my arm was starting to hurt from Laura twisting it, so I gave in. "One time," I said, "and that's all."

I was nervous about a few things and feared that Laura, in her zeal, had overlooked some important issues. I didn't have any golf clubs. Nor golf shoes. Nor proper golf attire. It was summer — in Phoenix, Arizona — which meant we'd be playing in triple-digit temperatures. I have an artificial knee as the result of a serious soccer injury in college. Oh, and I was pregnant. Do they have bathrooms at the golf course? A *lot* of bathrooms?

Although I was tempted to bail out, I called my mom and asked whether she had any golf clubs in her garage. She called back moments later. "They're dusty. And you'll still need a **Driver**." This news gave me a boost, because it seemed things were starting to go my way — I didn't need a Driver; Laura said we'd be using **pull carts**. I just needed comfortable shoes. It didn't occur to me that a Driver is a golf club.

Finding something to wear wasn't the problem I expected it to be. I had only to dress respectfully. We weren't going to a fashion show, for goodness sake. Shorts with pockets for my tissues? *Check.* Collared shirt light enough to be comfortable in the heat — and big enough to cover a pregnant woman's belly? *Looking... in husband's closet... check.*

On game day I arrived at downtown Phoenix's 9-hole Encanto **Executive Course** right on time. Or so I thought. In the **clubhouse**, as I paid my **green fee**, the cashier instructed me to hurry to join my group on the first tee. *Group?*

I ran, clubs rattling in the pull cart behind me. I was all arms and legs and belly. And high-top sneakers. And my husband's billowing polo shirt. My group — Laura and three male co-workers — watched my approach, awed. I had no idea, of course, that I was a fifth wheel!

Golf is typically played in **foursomes**.

That day, I learned that golfers enjoy introducing the game to newcomers and making it a fun experience. They delight in teaching you the language of golf and use gentle humor to put you at ease.

My first shot went 30 yards and disappeared into a thicket of oleander. *(I made contact! Woo-hoo!)* Big Phil from Atlanta, a country boy with the sweetest southern drawl I'd ever heard, followed me to the thicket to help look for my ball.

"Do y'all have a **foot wedge** in your bag, Miss Debbie?" he asked. I was sure I did because, according to my mother, all I was missing was a Driver. I searched through the clubs in vain. I found numbered clubs, an "SW" and a "PW," but no "FW." I looked up in dismay. Big Phil grinned and kicked my ball into the **fairway**. "There ya go, Miss Debbie. That's a foot wedge."

More than twenty-five years have passed since that day. I still recall everything about it. How beautiful the course was with all its green fairways, palm trees and flowering oleanders! How amazing it was to be hitting golf balls in a setting surrounded by the city. How profoundly it enhanced my already good working relationships with three male colleagues whose superior I was at the office! Most of all, I recall how much *fun* it was. Laura was right. I did love it.

Turn Golf into Gold

In 2000 I left my position as president of a firm in the corporate financial world to create *Golf for Cause*®, a company that focuses on helping organizations and individuals use golf as a tool to raise money, forward relationships and promote personal growth. Thousands of golfers, many of them women and a large percentage of them new golfers, have participated in various Golf for Cause workshops, conferences, clinics, tournaments, leagues and just-for-fun events to learn how to *turn golf into gold*®.

Charitable fundraising is gold, yes. And so much more than that. There is the gold that is a richness of friendships, of personal and business relationships, of bonding and teambuilding. The gold that is quality time spent with people you care about. The gold that fills your vault of treasured memories. The gold that is a connection with nature that yields a continuing harvest of invaluable insight and self-discovery.

Regardless how well you play, how often you play, where you play or whether you play at all, golf is a gold-laden game that can take you places you never thought you'd see and introduce you to people and experiences you never imagined possible.

Words of Wisdom

"Today we're all running 24-7. Some people believe they don't have time to play golf. But there's no rule that says you have to play 9 holes or 18 holes. Play 3 or 4 holes if that's all you have time for, or maybe just do some chipping and putting. What's important is to get out there. Put aside a little time to do it. I encourage people to play golf because it gives us something that can help us in our daily lives — the peacefulness of the golf course. Leave the phone in the car. Feel the sunshine. Smell the green grass. Listen to the birds singing. Soak in it and breathe.

"Of course, many people who play golf struggle with consistency because they aren't playing often enough. But they shouldn't be too hard on themselves. When you're playing twice a month or every three weeks, your goal should be to hit a good shot, and then another good shot. When you do hit a good shot, be excited about it, happy about it, even if it is only one shot out of ten. Enjoy the effort and embrace that you hit a good one. It's proof you can do it, and if you play more often you'll do it more often and develop consistency. That's your goal — hit one good shot and you'll keep coming back to the golf course to hit more of them."

Nancy Lopez
Nancy Lopez Golf Adventures
LPGA
World Golf Hall of Fame Inductee (1987)

As LPGA Co-Founder Shirley Spork Sees It...

Shirley Spork was there at the beginning, one of the thirteen visionary women who threw in with each other to co-found the Ladies Professional Golf Association. She was 23 years old. A marvelous lifetime later, Shirley can tell you a lot of things about this game and how to enjoy it.

"The top three best things about playing golf," she says, "are spending time in the beautiful out of doors; gaining self-confidence through accomplishing a goal; and enjoying the camaraderie." Leaving the office behind to experience nature for a few hours. *Check.* Personal growth. *Check.* Hanging with friends. *Check.* Your top three best things may be a little different, but these are hard to beat.

"The best single piece of advice I can offer every new golfer is to secure basic fundamentals from your local LPGA or PGA Golf Professional." Lessons. *Check.* "Golf is a game that provides a challenge. Having a grasp of the basic fundamentals enables you to meet the challenge, and meeting the challenge successfully is how you improve yourself." Pretty sound advice from the lady who helped establish the LPGA's Teaching Division, was twice named the LPGA National Teacher of the Year, and in 2000 was a member of the inaugural class of inductees into the LPGA Teaching and Club Professional Hall of Fame.

As Shirley looks back fondly over the excellent adventure that has been her life with golf, the memories of her experiences come forward pleasantly. Her best experience doesn't lie in the past. "My best experience in the sport of golf happens each time I see the enthusiastic smiles my pupils show." Spoken like a teacher. "Seeing their achievement is my reward as a coach, teacher, and friend. The numerous phone calls, pictures, and letters they send thanking me make me feel proud to be a teacher."

Here's another one, Shirley. Thank YOU!

Shirley Spork received the Byron Nelson Award in 1994, and in 2015 was the recipient of the Patty Berg Award, which recognizes an individual for outstanding contributions to women's golf. Now 92, Shirley remains active in golf and continues to provide lessons to a select few. You can find her book, From Green to Tee *on Amazon.*

It's Never Too Late

"I came to golf later in life and dearly wish I had been able to do it sooner. I had no awareness of golf's ability to pull people in and to be such a powerful platform for creating relationships—not just casual friendships but lasting, meaningful relationships. Golf is a game changer when it comes to making and developing connections. It has given me so many opportunities to spend time on the course with executives that I never would have interacted with otherwise. In the boardroom, it has allowed me to quickly establish bonds and build credibility that would have taken years to achieve. On a personal level, most of our best friends are people we either met on the golf course or end up with us on the golf course. I can't think of a more rewarding way to enrich your life than playing golf. You meet the best of humanity, and there's an added bonus—you're surrounded by the beautiful serenity of Nature."

Yvette Gonzales
C-Level Executive, Fortune 500 company

Chapter

2

You Can
Say That Again!

"One can never consent to creep
when one feels an impulse to soar."

~ Helen Keller

You hear the funniest things on a golf course. Some words and expressions don't seem to make sense, because they mean one thing on the course and something entirely different in everyday usage.

Take the scoring, for example. **Par** is the score that a skilled golfer can be expected to make on a hole. Par is good! Even better is to be under par. One less than par is called a **birdie**. Two less than par is called an **eagle**. And while it is rare, three less than par is an **albatross** (the lower the score the bigger the bird). One more than par is a **bogey**. Two more than par is a **double bogey**. So remember, in golf, being par for the course is a good thing. Being sub-par (under par) is a really good thing!

Golf language can be quite colorful, too, and jargon varies from geographical region to geographical region. Making up new words is always encouraged and can create wonderful memories.

Golf has its share of four-letter words, even an "F" word. That word is **"FORE!"** You shout this word as loud as you can when you hit a shot that looks as if it may hit another golfer. There's an "S" word, too — our "S" word is "special" — and it means the same thing that other "S" word does. Ours is just a nicer way of saying it.

I'm not encouraging profanity here. Tension can be very destructive to your attitude and your swing. When you hit one of those wayward shots, keep an eye on where it goes and simply declare, "Wasn't that special." Not only will you find some humor in it and put the rest of your foursome at ease, you'll help yourself let go of any negativity. Try it! I suspect you'll say the "S" word with a smile!

You've already noticed that some words in this book are in **bold**. These words and others are in the golf lingo glossary at the back of the book. Check it out for a listing of golf 's descriptive and often clever terminology. Most of them are self-explanatory, although you may have to think about them for a moment. A few are part of golf 's lexicon despite making no sense to anyone. **Duck hook**, for example, describes a right-handed golfer's shot when it curves sharply from right to left and stays low to the ground. "Hook" is understand-able. "Duck," not so much. But you'll hear it.

Golfers talk less to each other than they talk to themselves, their golf balls, the sky, God and even invisible people. But it is all in fun and there is actually a good reason for it: you release the frustration that sometimes comes when you hit a ball that doesn't go where you hoped it would.

Mention Golf and a Conversation Starts

"My ex and I used to go out and hack around at a golf course, and I'd play when asked, but it was always just about being outdoors and having a beer. After my divorce I started playing with my sister and brother-in-law at a course near their time-share in Arizona, because I thought it might be a nice way to meet men. Of course I didn't want to embarrass myself, so I took six lessons from the golf professional. Now I am the instigator of playing golf!

"I created Dunn Transportation to get more involved in the business of golf. Our executive coaches are designed to transport as many as 36 passengers — or 6 foursomes — and their golf bags (bags are kept upright, mind you). But I play golf to have fun and laugh my $%#&! off. It's a great way to meet people and a great way to break the ice. Mention that you play golf and a conversation starts."

Margaret Dunn
Owner, Atypical Transportation Company
Dunn Transportation Company

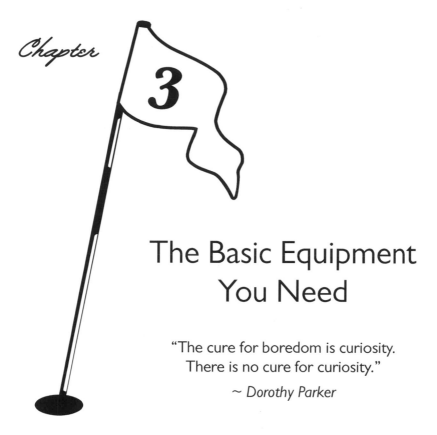

The Basic Equipment You Need

"The cure for boredom is curiosity.
There is no cure for curiosity."

~ *Dorothy Parker*

To play golf, you need equipment, same as any other sport. Baseball, you need a bat and a ball. Tennis, a racket and a ball. Golf, clubs and a ball. *Clubs? More than one? Yes.* In golf, you need a variety of clubs to obtain a variety of results. The way the ball flies through the air when you hit it depends on which club you use. This is one of the reasons hitting golf balls can be so much fun.

Golf Clubs

Some golf newcomers find "the whole golf club thing" confusing. So let's begin with a few simple observations:

- Every player must have a golf bag with golf clubs in it.
- The golf bag can have up to 14 clubs, but no more.
- New golfers typically don't need all 14 clubs to start in the game.

- There are clubs for left-hand golfers and clubs for righties.
- There are clubs for women and clubs for men (although some women prefer to play with men's clubs).
- Clubs come in different lengths. The shorter the club, the shorter it sends the ball.

Sandy's advice on clubs:

Sandy LaBauve is a Top 100 PGA and LPGA teaching professional and Founder of LPGA*USGA Girls Golf. She is passionate about growing the game of golf by empowering others. She encourages you to advocate for yourself when you're shopping for golf clubs. Order what you want. Similar to what you do with the clothes in your closet, put in what you want and clear out what you don't wear. For your golf bag, put in only the clubs that you'll use.

Asked for specific advice about what to put in your golf bag, Sandy says, "I am a true believer that driving clubs need to go as far as possible but stay in play. With current technology, drivers are easier to hit today because they are lightweight and come in a variety of lofts. Pick a driver that works for you. The average range in loft is 9-13 degrees. Many drivers even have an adjustable loft. This is beneficial because you can change the loft as your skills improve. Start with more loft because you can carry the ball farther in the air and it will fly straighter. Loft is your friend.

"A driver's job is to launch the ball off of a tee, sending it a reasonable distance, with the ball landing in the width of the fairway. If you can't hit your ball with a driver and keep it in the fairway or close to the edge, select a club that will keep your ball in play. Remember, loft is your friend!

"You will probably have to hit one or two long advancement clubs such as a 7-wood or a 5-hybrid to move your ball down the fairway.

"The closer you get to the hole, the shorter the shot you have to play. Your precision clubs are the 8-iron, 9-iron, wedges and putter. I call them 'Precision clubs' because you're aiming at a more precise target and want to get as close as you can to that target. That's also why you should practice these clubs more than your other clubs.

"You typically get to make a partial swing with a lofted club for shorter shots. Make sure you have the tools to hit these shots. I recommend carrying at least 3 wedges. Become skilled with these shots quickly because you will have to hit them frequently. Along with your putter, they are your scoring clubs."

Set make-ups for most women coming into the game vary. You're allowed to have 14 clubs in your bag, but consider having just these 10:

- High-lofted Driver
- A 5- or 7-Wood (sometimes referred to as a "Fairway Metal" – if you're athletic the 5 might be more suitable for you than the 7)
- Two Hybrid Clubs (also called Rescue Clubs)
- 8-Iron
- 9-Iron
- Pitching Wedge
- Utility Wedge (also called an "A," "Gap" or "Dual" Wedge)
- Sand Wedge
- Putter

Some golf club manufacturers offer a full set (14 clubs) as well as a "partial" or "basic" set of clubs, which contains fewer than 14 clubs. These sets might even include a golf bag!

NOTE: A typical full set of men's clubs consists of a driver, 3-wood, 5-wood, hybrid, 4-, 5-, 6-, 7-, 8- & 9-irons, 3 wedges and a putter. There can be variations in the make up of a set.

So many clubs, so many choices! Why?

Different clubs send the golf ball different distances and give it different trajectories. Here's an easy way to understand the numbers on the clubs: the higher the number, the higher the ball trajectory and the shorter the distance the ball goes (and also the shorter distance it rolls after it lands). Another way to look at it is this: picture a child playing with a garden hose, trying to soak someone nearby. Raising the hose to make the water go higher SHORTENS the distance it travels. Also, the water hits the ground with a splat and doesn't get much farther. The same principle applies to your golf clubs: use a higher number club and the result is a higher, shorter shot.

Today, many golf club manufacturers print the degree of loft on the club, which makes it even easier to determine which club you want to use. A sand wedge, for example, is 56°, so the ball should go high, but not far. A driver, at 12°, will make the ball fly lower and much farther than the sand wedge.

You are allowed to carry any combination of clubs you desire, up to 14 clubs, in your golf bag. Although these combinations are impractical, you could choose to carry only two drivers and nothing else, or four wedges, or 14 putters — any combination.

Very often, new golfers start out with golf clubs borrowed from a friend or relative. This is a perfectly acceptable, financially sound decision, but a strong word of caution:

> Men's golf clubs are heavier than women's clubs. They typically have stiffer, steel shafts rather than lighter-weight graphite shafts, and the shafts may be longer. All of this works to a woman's disadvantage, is detrimental to performance and enjoyment, and can be exhausting, as well. If you are a woman and borrow clubs, try to borrow a woman's set.

Also, when you borrow clubs, it is likely that they are someone's old or second set. Beggars can't be choosers, but golf club manufacturing technology continues to improve club quality and performance, so much so that clubs only a few years old won't help you play your best.

Borrowing or renting clubs allows you to get a feel for the game before you incur the expense of purchasing your own clubs. When you do decide to buy clubs, I strongly encourage you to buy them from a store or golf facility that will "fit" you to your clubs.

You'll read more about golf clubs and **club fitting** in Chapter 5, *Let's Go To The Driving Range*.

Golf Bag

You need a golf bag in which to carry your clubs. There are many styles and brands of bags to choose from. Some bags are designed for golfers who prefer to walk when they play, as opposed to riding in a golf cart. These bags are lighter weight, have retractable "stand up" legs, and are usually smaller than "cart" bags, which are the choice of golfers who prefer riding to walking.

Every golf bag has pockets, and you may discover that the number of pockets is one of your most important considerations. You'll need a pocket for your golf balls, certainly, but you'll also want pockets for your golf tees, pencils, sunscreen, snacks, car keys, business cards, cell phone and perhaps even a water bottle and a light weight jacket.

Be sure to put your name on your golf bag. A luggage tag works great, or you can purchase one of the tags available at golf stores and pro shops.

NOTE: Two additional items to have with your golf bag are a ball retriever (a retractable tool to retrieve your ball from water or dense shrubbery when you make one of those "special" shots) and a golf towel for cleaning your clubs. Clean clubs perform better.

Golf Balls

As a new golfer, choosing the kind of golf balls you want to play may seem confusing when you see how many there are to choose from. It can be even more confusing if you read the blurbs on the boxes. So don't do that. My advice to new golfers is this: simply start with the least expensive balls. The kind of ball you play will only be a concern once your skill level improves significantly.

Some balls are marked "Ladies," but this has more to do with marketing than performance characteristics. If you look closely you will even see a particular brand of balls called "Laddies." Precept, the manufacturer, discovered that quite a few men were playing Precept "Ladies" balls because they went farther, yet the men felt a bit awkward about it. It was an easy problem to solve: the manufacturer changed the "Ladies" to "Laddies" and promoted the "new" ball.

You'll also notice that golf balls are available in colors other than white. If you like pink, great. Orange or yellow or lime green? Great. Whatever you like is fine.

How many golf balls should you carry in your bag? Most golfers carry a dozen, plus or minus a few.

And That Was My Last Time in the "Spa Group"

"I had always heard about business getting done on the golf course, and I had considered that I should take up golf, but I was always in school. The law firm I joined was exactly what I was looking for. The only catch was that I would be the only female lawyer. This did not bother me in the least. My first attorney retreat was about 5 weeks after I started with the firm. I received an agenda for the weekend, planned by our female administrator, and glanced over the activities — group functions, dinners with spouses and spa appointments. I looked at my husband's itinerary and saw some of the same group functions, the dinner and *golf*.

"After distributing the itineraries, the administrator approached me and said she had booked a tee time for my husband with the men and an appointment for me at the spa with the wives. She asked if this was okay and suggested she could change it if necessary. I agreed to keep my spa appointment to make things easy — but I was committed that never again would I be in the spa group."

Stephanie McCoy Loquvam
Attorney At Law

I Realized the Boys Were Doing Business

"For me it was necessity. I think many women golfers get started out of necessity. I was working in a mostly male, certainly male-dominated banking environment. My title and responsibilities were the same as the men in the office, but I wasn't 'one of the guys.' The guys would come back to the office after a round of golf and they'd be talking about things I hadn't been privy to. Things I needed to know. I realized that they weren't just playing golf—they were doing business, too. I needed to get in the game.

Maurine Karabatsos
Founder and Chief Strategist
QR GamePlan

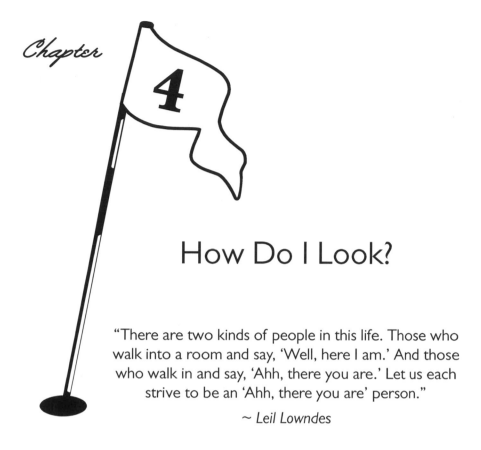

4

How Do I Look?

"There are two kinds of people in this life. Those who walk into a room and say, 'Well, here I am.' And those who walk in and say, 'Ahh, there you are.' Let us each strive to be an 'Ahh, there you are' person."

~ *Leil Lowndes*

If you love clothes and fashion, you will love shopping for golf attire. Golf clothing is designed for fashion and function. Looking like a golfer will help you feel like a golfer. But it isn't a rule that you have to wear clothes specifically designed for golf. Wardrobe rules are very simple, in fact:

- Almost all golf courses require collared shirts for men.
- Women's shirts, if sleeveless, must have a collar; if the shirt has sleeves, no collar is necessary.
- Shorts are fine, but not short shorts.
- Denim anything is a no-no.
- Sneakers are okay if you don't have golf shoes.

Shorts, skorts, capris and slacks should have pockets large enough to put your hand into. The first time I played golf I chose to wear shorts with pockets because I needed a place to put my tissues. I didn't realize I'd need pockets for other things — an extra ball, a few **tees**, a **ball marker**, and a **divot repair tool**.

Have fun with your wardrobe. Just remember that you'll be bending over a lot, squatting, twisting your body and raising your arms.

Glove It

Glove It is a fabulous line of fun golf and active lifestyle accessories. Whether you play golf well or not as well as you'd like, you always want to look great!

Glove It offers a fabulous, well-coordinated product line in fun prints and styles, from traditional argyles to animal prints — something to match every outfit in your closet!

The Glove It collection includes quality leather golf gloves, visors, accessory bags, club covers, shoe bags, golf bags, towels and more!

Shop online at www.gloveit.com

Hats, Caps and Visors

Yes! Always bring something to protect your head from the sun and elements.

Golf Glove

Most golfers prefer to wear a glove because they feel it helps them grip the club. You may prefer to not wear a glove. But keep this in mind:

- A right-handed golfer wears the glove on his/her LEFT hand.
- A left-handed golfer wears the glove on his/her RIGHT hand.

Wearing the glove on the "wrong" hand will make sense to you when you start hitting balls.

Some players wear gloves on both hands for sun protection. And there are rain gloves that you'll want to wear on both hands when you play in those conditions.

Note that some golf gloves have a ball marker that you can use on the green integrated right into their design.

Golf Shoes

When you buy golf shoes, be sure they are very comfortable — you'll be doing a lot of walking. There are many great styles and colors to choose from, but comfort is your most important consideration.

Many golf shoes have removable soft spikes (virtually all golf courses no longer allow the old-fashioned metal spikes), but not all spikes fit all shoes. When your spikes are worn down and need to be replaced, bring one of the spikes or one of your shoes to the store to be sure you get the right type. Also, it is a good idea to check the tightness of spikes on new shoes — sometimes the factory ships them untightened. (It takes a special tool to tighten them, but if you don't have one, the golf shops will always assist you.)

You'll also see some golf shoes that are spikeless, sporting nubs on their bottoms that do not need to be replaced. They're quite comfortable and very acceptable to wear on the golf course. While golf shoes with nubs are comfortable and easy to wear as street shoes, resist the urge to wear them away from the golf course as the nubs will wear down more quickly.

NOTE: New shoes may cause blisters. Be prepared: keep a few Band-Aids®, blister bandages or moleskin in your golf bag. If you need a Band-Aid and don't have one, ask in the pro shop — they can almost always help you.

Jack Grace Golf Shoes

One fun brand of golf shoes is Jack Grace USA. The shoes have nubs on the bottom and the color selection is endless.

They are saddle shoes that you can swap out the saddle to match any outfit in your closet! They're waterproof and very comfortable, too!

Visit www.JackGraceUSA.com

ƀ
JACK GRACE

Wardrobe Extras

Depending on the weather, you may want to put a windbreaker or sweater in your golf bag. A golf umbrella can also come in handy, so if it looks like rain is a possibility, take one. Plus, the umbrella can help provide shade on warm, sunny days. Most golf bags have a special umbrella holder on the outside of the bag.

I Couldn't Find a Thing to Wear

We all have said it, haven't we? Sometimes just to be funny. But for women who play golf, it used to be quite a problem. I was fortunate to grow up in a family that lived and breathed sports; yet, I didn't really get interested in playing golf until my late 20s when I married a man who encouraged me to take it up so we could enjoy the game together. I took lessons because anything worth doing is worth doing right. The problem for me was finding things to wear that not only were comfortable and functional but fashionable. This became an especially challenging issue for me in my professional life. As one of the few C-level executive women in corporate America working in strategic marketing for the healthcare industry at the time, I had many opportunities to play golf with clients on some of the finest courses in the country. I could purchase golf attire in the pro shops, but there was always a chance I'd get to a golf course and find that I was dressed just like someone else. Something had to be done!

At the *Masters* golf tournament nearly a decade ago I launched the online business *Golf4Her* to give women a real choice when it comes to outfitting for golf. Today we are the "go to" shop for thousands of female golfers, from beginning golfers to weekend players like us to LPGA professionals. If you are looking for the very latest collections that combine performance and style, you'll find it all in our online pro shop. And if you don't like shopping online, we recently opened our first retail shop. If you're in Denville, New Jersey come see us!

You've heard it said countless times that golf is a game that opens doors for you. You bet it does. And now you can always look on point driving through them!

Christina Thompson
Founder and CEO
Golf4Her
www.golf4her.com

5

Let's Go to the Driving Range

"Don't be afraid to look unfeminine by taking a whole-hearted whack with the club. Anyone strong enough to lift a two-year-old child or tote a vacuum cleaner or a bag of groceries can hit a powerful shot."

~ Sharron Moran

You have clubs. You look like a golfer. Now you need to hit some balls to get comfortable with your clubs — keeping in mind the old saying, "Practice makes perfect." So let's go to the driving range!

Most golf courses have driving ranges or practice areas that are separate from the golf course. This means that you can pay for a bucket of practice balls without having to pay a green fee as you would for playing 9 or 18 holes.

Most cities have stand-alone driving ranges that are not connected to a golf course. These practice facilities often have lights for nighttime practice — a nice way to spend an hour after work or later in the evening! Also, driving ranges are great places to meet people and make new friends.

Here are a few things to think about before you get to the driving range:

The driving range is a place to have fun in a casual setting while you are getting familiar with your golf clubs — figuring out how you grip them; how you position yourself to hit the ball (how you **"address"** it); how you swing; and how far the ball goes depending on which club you use.

After you purchase a small or large bucket (or basket or bag) of balls (usually from $5 - $12 per bucket), take the bucket and your golf clubs to the practice area where other golfers are practicing. You may want to take only a few clubs with you rather than your whole bag.

A note about purchasing practice balls: depending on where you go, you may be handed a bucket of balls, or you may be given a receipt to show the outside attendant or a token to put in a machine that will spit out balls into a bucket. The balls may already be at the hitting area. In any case, keep your receipt handy, as you may have to show it to someone. If you have to get the balls from a machine, BE SURE TO PUT THE BUCKET UNDER THE DISPENSER FIRST. If you forget to do this, 50 –100 golf balls will spill out and go all over the place. And it wouldn't be the first time *that's* happened!

Before you start hitting balls, always be sure to do a few minutes of stretching exercises to loosen your body and warm up your muscles. This is very important at the driving range because, here, you are hitting balls at a much faster pace than when you are playing golf on a course.

While you are warming up, observe the other golfers. Quite often the people hitting balls are accomplished golfers, so you can learn by watching them. Note how they grip their clubs, bend their knees, position their feet, hold their heads, and swing. When you see a golfer hitting nice shot after nice shot, that's a good golfer to watch. If you feel awkward studying someone's form and swing, ask if he or she is okay with it.

Synthetic Turf Mats

Most golfers prefer practicing on real grass, but some practice facilities may ask at times that you to hit off synthetic turf mats. This won't hurt you, it isn't what you experience on real grass. Also, you may find a small rubber tube sticking up on the left or right side of the synthetic mats. This acts as a tee.

Which Club to Hit First?

Start with a wedge. It is the shortest and most lofted of your clubs and will give you an opportunity to ease into your swings. Take note of the colored flags in the landing area in front of you. Choose one as your target and try to hit toward it consistently.

Always watch where your ball lands, because you are on an important mission: by trying out your different clubs, you are seeking to identify which one is your "100-yard club." Be patient with yourself, because your swing is not yet repeating (meaning that it's not yet the same, swing after swing after swing). You may have to go to the practice range several times before you can determine which club is your 100-yard club.

Your 100-Yard Club: The Key to the Kingdom — Er, Queendom

Once you have determined which of your clubs makes the ball go approximately 100 yards, you've made a HUGE advance in your golf game. How huge? Paraphrasing the immortal words of Neil Armstrong, it's one small step, one giant leap. Here's why:

You now know how far you can hit the ball with each iron in your bag, which is critically important to know when you are playing a round of golf. You'll read more about this in Chapter 8, *Understanding Scorecards And Course Guides*.

If your 100-yard club is the 7-iron, add 10 yards for each club lower than the 7-iron, and subtract 10 yards for each club higher than the 7-iron. Using that formula, estimate that your 6-iron will send the ball about 110 yards; your 5-hybrid, 120 yards. Going the other way, your 8-iron will send your ball about 90 yards; your 9-iron, about 80 yards.

For women, the difference in distance between each club is typically 10 yards. For men, it's 15 yards.

Woods are used to hit a golf ball farther than irons. Although now made of metal, the club heads were once made out of wood, and

the name has stuck even after the technological advancements. Occasionally, you might hear someone call them "metal woods" or "fairway metals."

There are generally three kinds of woods: **drivers, fairway woods**, and **hybrids**. The driver is considered the 1-wood. It's the longest club in your bag and, traditionally, for some golfers, the hardest club to control because the face has very little loft. However, with today's technological advances, the driver now has more loft and is easier to control. The most common fairway woods are the 3-wood, 5-wood and 7-wood. And, yes, you use them on the fairway as well as on the teeing area.

Hybrid clubs combine the characteristics of woods and irons. They can be used off the tee and in the fairway. Should you find yourself in the **rough** (the grass not in the fairway), you'll often find it easier to hit with your hybrid club than with a wood or an iron. If your set has a hybrid club or two, then it will probably not have one of the lower lofted irons, such as a 4, 5, or 6-iron.

hybrids

At the driving range, after hitting balls with your irons, hit a few balls off a tee using your hybrid club(s). Then, hit some with your fairway wood(s) and finish with your driver.

When you feel that you've hit enough balls for one day, but still have some remaining, just leave them for the next golfer. It's an act of kindness that's always appreciated (although practice facilities see it as a revenue loss).

Practice (Range) Balls –

Practice balls are either "seconds" that the manufacturer's quality control mechanism rejected or they are balls made specifically for driving range use. Some are even distance controlled. They are suitable for practice, but never use them to play on the golf course — they will make you look bad in every imaginable way.

"Drive for Show, Putt for Dough."

You'll hear this expression a million times, and that's fine. It underscores one of the great truths about golf: approximately half of your shots in a round of golf will be putts and short shots made from close to the green. It's true even for the pros. If you can improve your **putting** (and it's the easiest thing to improve!), it will help build your confidence. (And you thought miniature golf was just for goofing around!)

Be sure to allow time for working on your short game — **chipping**, **pitching** and putting. This is where you can make the biggest difference in your game.

Fitting Your Clubs

Like many beginning golfers, I started out with a borrowed set

Practice Facilities Vary Greatly –

*Some have only a driving range, while others have a range and a putting green. Still others have both and also a green for chipping and **bunker** practice. Before you start putting, be sure you aren't on the chipping green — you'll be bombarded!*

of clubs. They had steel shafts and were too long for me, but I didn't know steel shafts make golf clubs heavier, nor that club lengths vary. So I didn't know they were affecting my swing. I was just swinging away, happy as I could be. Also, like many new golfers, I was taking an excessive number of practice swings before every shot. No wonder I was thinking golf is a calorie-burning workout!

There are some golf equipment professionals who believe you should get custom-fit clubs from the beginning. They point out that you aren't likely to wear size 10 shoes if you have size 8 feet. Can't argue with that. The same argument applies to bowling balls — if you've ever bowled you know how important it is to have a ball that fits your fingers and is the perfect weight.

The key to golf is having a repeatable swing — a swing motion that for the most part remains unchanged swing after swing after swing. Once you have one, you might consider investing in a set of clubs that are crafted with the latest technology and custom fit to your exact needs. A club fitter will evaluate the length that's right for you, the flexibility of the shaft, your swing speed, the thickness of the grip, the lie angle (as you stand with the club in your hands, this is the angle between the shaft and the sole of the club), even the trajectory of the ball when you hit it.

Finding a club fitter is easy. Simply ask your golf professional, your friends, anyone in a golf shop, or look online.

Club fitting doesn't give you a bag of magic wands — custom fit clubs won't take care of a poor swing technique, but they will certainly help you hit the ball more solidly, more confidently and more accurately. Plus, you'll love that they're yours!

Banking on Golf for Professional Survival

"I started playing in the mid-1980s when I saw the strong connection between business and golf and realized I needed to get in the game, so to speak. To me it seemed a matter of professional survival. My first experience was playing in a scramble with borrowed clubs, and we got a trophy!"

Gail Grace
Retired Bank President

Gail has won a lot of trophies since then — her office is filled with trophies and framed photos of her tournament foursomes. A special treasure is a framed Moon Valley Country Club flag signed by Annika Sorenstam the day she carded a tournament-record 59 there.

6

Scheduling (Reserving) a Tee Time

"A ship in a harbor is safe,
but that is not what ships are built for."

~ *William Shedd*

New golfers often say that once they get on the golf course and actually play, that's when they realize they love the game. You're ready to find out if that's true for you. You've been practicing. You're comfortable with your clubs and relatively comfortable with your swing. You feel ready to have a go at playing a round of golf with two or three friends. All you need now is a tee time.

Reserving tee times is *reeeeeeeally* easy. You can do it in person, by phone or online. Online options include your local golf course's website and online golf services such as *golfnow.com* and *teeoff.com*.

Before you attempt to reserve your tee time, determine how many golfers will be in your group. The maximum number allowed is usually four, or a foursome. (My first outing, as part of a fivesome, is quite rare.) Often you will find that courses don't want to reserve a tee time for a party of one. Also note that if you book a tee time for a twosome, the course will very likely put one or two other golfers with you when you arrive. Ideally, a group of four friends is the way to go — especially when you are just learning to play.

Some golf courses will ask you for a credit card to hold your tee time reservation. If you fail to show up and do not cancel in advance, you may be charged for your **green fee**.

Tee times are typically spaced 8 – 10 minutes apart, so if you want to play at, say, noon, you may get an 11:52 a.m. time or a 12:08 p.m. time if noon is unavailable. During the busy season, the course may be booked completely, in which case you will have to try a different course or a different day. Fridays, Saturdays and Sundays are the busiest days. Some courses may charge a higher green fee for weekend tee times and include Fridays as part of the weekend.

Pay close attention to the EXACT time that is reserved for you, and be sure to tell your playing partners the EXACT tee time. You'll see why this is so important when you get to the next chapter.

When you book your tee time online, be sure to check the course's website for special offers. Many courses offer discounted green fees to customers who book online and occasionally offer breakfast/golf or golf/

Canceling Your Tee Time –

Most courses allow you to cancel your tee time without penalty if you give 24 hours' notice. Always check the course's cancellation policy, particularly with regard to RAIN. If it rains and you don't show up for your tee time, you MAY get charged the full amount.

lunch promotions. One disadvantage of booking online, however, is that you don't have an opportunity to inquire if the golf course is appropriate for your skill level as well as what condition the course is in. Necessary seasonal maintenance such as **punching** won't close the course, but it can certainly detract from your playing enjoyment.

It will take you approximately 4.5 hours to play 18 holes of golf.

Pace of Play

Pace of play is a fast igniter of spirited discussion for amateur and professional golfers alike. Everyone has an opinion about it, and everyone agrees — slow is no way to play.

As a new golfer, you might worry that your skill level will make it difficult for you to keep up with other, more experienced players. You may even fear it could cost you another invitation to play. If you're playing with clients or coworkers, you might even be concerned that it could indirectly cost you money, too! That's a reality for professionals! They can be penalized and may even be fined.

Put your mind at ease. There are no speed limit signs on the golf course and keeping up with the pace of play is not hard at all. Here are six tips that will help you keep up and create an enjoyable experience (do these things and you could even play with the biggest names in professional golf):

1. Don't worry about the group behind you; focus on keeping up with the group ahead.

2. On the green, stand by your ball so you're ready to play when it's your turn. Line-up your putt while the others are putting, being careful to not distract them.

3. Mark the scorecard when you reach the next hole. You don't want to get hit by incoming balls, and you'll have time at the next hole while your playing partners are selecting clubs and teeing off.

4. When you must walk to your ball, take an extra club or two. If you think you need a 7-iron, take your 6 and 8-iron too. This is called "bracketing." If you're close to the green, take your putter. Your playing partner can drive the cart to the green.

5. If using a cart, don't put your club away after hitting. Hang onto it and drive or ride to the next shot. When you step out of the cart again, put your club back in the bag.

6. If you are really worried about falling behind, just pick up your ball to keep up! As a new or seasoned recreational golfer, it is

always ok to pick your ball up and drop it closer to the green or near another playing partner's ball. Finish the hole by putting with everyone else.

Use these tips and you'll be able to play with anyone — without worrying about causing a slowdown! And the odds are high that you'll be invited to play again and again.

My Great Escape

"I used to be just a vacation player. I would ride in the cart with my husband and, if we came to a hole I could hit on, I'd get out and hit or putt.

"My husband has been playing since he was young. One day he said that if I'd take up golf, we could join a club — it didn't make sense to join a club for just one person. So I started playing.

"I love the game and love the people I play with. The camaraderie is wonderful. On the golf course, I don't think about anything other than hitting the $%#&! ball — not my house, not my business, not the kids. Golf takes me away from everything."

Helen Burland
Owner, Burland Jewelers

Golf, the Great Giver

"The game of golf has truly given me everything I value in life. Everything. It was a treasured way to spend time with my father and bond with my family when I was growing up in Nebraska. Later it gave me a ride to Southern California and an education at a prestigious Division I university. It presented me a way to build a successful career, and brought me the opportunity to meet my wonderful husband. And now it rewards us with countless special memories that we are creating with our children. I just don't think there is another sport that can match golf's ability to give these gifts and enrich a person's life so completely."

Jill Mann Strite
Versatile Golf
Owner and LPGA Class A Professional

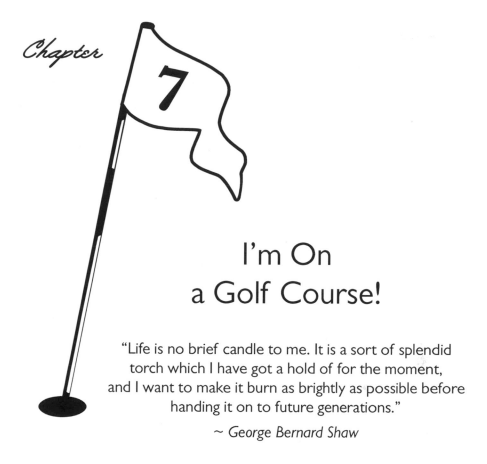

Chapter

I'm On a Golf Course!

"Life is no brief candle to me. It is a sort of splendid torch which I have got a hold of for the moment, and I want to make it burn as brightly as possible before handing it on to future generations."

~ *George Bernard Shaw*

This is the day! For the first time, you are going to play 9 or 18 holes. Excited?

Your tee time is 12:08 p.m. The **starter** will give you about 5 minutes notice. 12:08 p.m. is the exact time you are expected to hit your first ball. (If there is no starter, you are expected to be on the tee at your designated time.) You'll want to warm up before you play, and you'll need a little time to pay your green fee, shop in the pro shop, grab something from the snack bar, and get your group together and not feel rushed so ARRIVE AT THE COURSE AT LEAST 45 MINUTES BEFORE YOUR TEE TIME.

The Bag Drop

When you arrive at the golf course, look for a **Bag Drop** sign near the entrance to the clubhouse. This is where you stop long enough to give your clubs to one of the attendants before parking your car. The attendant will welcome you, ask for your name and tee time, then put your clubs on a cart. Be sure to ask the attendant where your clubs will be when you exit the pro shop. At the end of your round it is appropriate to tip the attendant a few dollars that would include this service. It isn't required to tip when you drop off your golf clubs. Note that private courses might not allow any tipping.

Some golf courses have locker rooms where you can change into your golf shoes, put on sunscreen, etc. It is considered good etiquette to put on your shoes inside the locker room clubhouse or restroom as opposed to changing in the parking lot.

The Pro Shop

The friendliest people on earth work in golf course pro shops. They are absolutely committed to helping YOU have a great time at their facility because they want you to come back, and they hope you'll tell others about it. Enjoy the attention!

A staff member behind the counter will check you in for your tee time. Be sure to save your receipt and put it where you can find it — the starter may ask to see it when you are called to the first tee or may even collect it from you.

If you are riding, the green fee covers the cost of the cart. If you are walking, the green fee will be less. Some courses discourage walking because the distance between holes can be quite long. Some courses may have pull carts that walking golfers can rent for a nominal fee as an alternative to carrying their bags. If you want to hit some practice balls before you play, there may be a small cost for a basket or bag of warm-up balls, or it might be included in your green fee.

Do you have plenty of golf balls in your bag? A towel? Sunscreen? A glove? A divot repair tool? A ball marker? Now's the time to get anything you need.

Waiting to Tee Off

You'll probably want to hit a few balls to warm up and you should practice putting, too, to get a feel for how your ball will roll on the putting green. This is an ideal time for you to count your golf clubs. Be sure that you have all of them and that you do not have more than 14.

About 10 minutes before your tee time, you should be in your cart and ready to go. If you are driving the cart, you will keep score, because the scorecard is on the steering wheel. As a new golfer, however, you have enough going on as it is, so try to let someone else drive the cart and keep score. You'll read about keeping score

Pro Shop Love at First Sight

I'll tell you what it is like to be behind the counter in the Pro Shop when a new golfer comes in. If I hear you say, "It's my first time here," that's music to my ears. Maybe it's your first time ever in a pro shop, or maybe just the first time in my pro shop. Either way, it's a great icebreaker and deserves a little extra pro shop attention and love. New golfers give us the opportunity to brag about our facility and explain a few basic things such as how to get to the golf carts, and where the driving range and practice areas are located. We want to put you at ease and create a flawless, smooth experience. Every course and clubhouse is different, but I think I'm speaking for most of the people in our industry— seeing somebody new in the pro shop is kind of exciting. We want your experience to be so good you'll come back. One more thing… if you have a question you're afraid to ask because you think it might be silly, there's no such thing. We love them all!

Rich Strozewski
Managing Partner
Springfield Golf Resort

in Chapter 8, *Understanding Scorecards and Course Guides.* (Relax — keeping score is easy!)

A Few Words About Golf Course Etiquette

This is the topic many new golfers are most concerned about, but let me put you at ease. Golf etiquette can be summed up in two words: be courteous. As a new golfer, the most courteous thing you can do is maintain a good pace of play and not prevent anyone from having a great day on the course. Keeping up a fast or reasonable pace of play is the one thing on the golf course that is totally within your control. This will also be the biggest factor in your popularity with your playing partners.

When a player in your group is preparing to hit her ball, position yourself behind her and to the side, outside her peripheral vision. (Think "bellies and backsides.") Remain still and quiet — you don't want to distract her or be the scapegoat should she make a "special" shot. When she hits her ball, watch where it goes so you can help locate it.

Most private golf clubs forbid the use of cell phones on the course, and most golfers, whether playing a private course or a public one, turn their phones OFF. In other words, be in the moment and be with your group. If you absolutely must check your messages, do it at **the turn**.

With that said, many golfers use their Smartphones for a variety of things that can enhance a round of golf — a golf app that provides a detailed hole information for a course, taking photos, posting photos to social media and even playing music. As a convenience, many facilities now have golf carts that have USB chargers. If you bring your cable, you can charge your Smartphone during your round.

A few words about music on the golf course. If you love to listen to music when you play golf, your playing partners might share your passion. Music certainly adds an element of fun and is no longer an uncommon part of playing golf. Before you take the liberty of playing some songs, you should absolutely inquire whether your playing partners mind listening to music on the golf course. If they do, then don't turn on your music. You wouldn't want to be the reason that a player decides she's distracted. If the others in your group don't mind having music, enjoy — just make sure you're not sharing your tunes with those on the next hole, the next fairway or another group.

The key ring on the cart may have two keys. The bigger key is for the rest rooms (comfort stations! Yeah!) on the course.

comfort station

The golf cart has an ON/ OFF key and a forward- reverse control. This control may be a switch on the cart's dashboard or a lever on the seat bench between you and your playing partner.

How to Drive the Golf Cart

To make the cart go, step on the accelerator. There is no need to turn the key on and off. When you stop the cart, be sure to lock the brake by depressing the top portion of the brake pedal until it clicks.

Push top of pedal to lock brake

When you stop your cart behind another cart, as you will do each time you reach the teeing area for the next hole, always leave enough room between the carts to allow the front cart's golfers easy access to their clubs.

The starter at the golf course or the staff in the staging area will usually tell you where you may and may not drive the cart. Sometimes you'll see a notice on the golf cart itself. Here are some common guidelines you may see:

- *Cart Path Only* – (typical when the course conditions are very wet or shortly after **overseeding**).

- *90-Degree Rule* – drive on the cart path, and when you near your ball, turn 90 degrees to approach it. After hitting, drive back to the cart path the way you came.

- *Scatter Rule* – you may drive anywhere in any direction.

Never Thought I Would Say It, But...

"I never thought I would say these words: I love golf! Today I confess I love everything about it. The fresh air, the varying topography, the walking, the Saturday morning camaraderie with my girlfriends, the rounds played with colleagues, clients or my husband, the fashion and outfits — and most of all, the challenge of the game. A game you can play practically anywhere in the world! Looking back a few years, I know one of the main reasons I decided to take up golf was because I thought I would like to see my husband in retirement. Another confession: At the end of the day, I have to say, I love the game for ME!"

Ann Lieff
Account Manager, People Solutions
HKMB HUB International

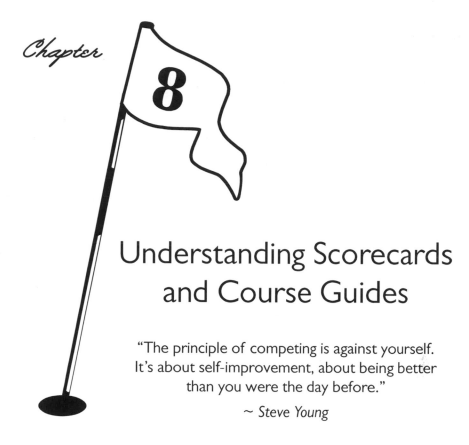

Chapter

8

Understanding Scorecards and Course Guides

"The principle of competing is against yourself. It's about self-improvement, about being better than you were the day before."

~ *Steve Young*

The key to your golf game is your 100-yard club, and the key to the golf course is the scorecard. Here's why:

> The scorecard tells you everything you need to know about the course — how long each hole is, how difficult each hole is compared to all the other holes, how difficult the course is compared to all other courses and how to make the scoring fair for each player in your group. The scorecard also informs you of any "Local Rules," such as what is considered **out of bounds**. It even gives the golf course's phone number, should you need it.

Take a look at the Scottsdale Silverado Golf Club scorecard. Reading from top to bottom, this is what it tells us:

> The course has 4 sets of tees for each hole — gold, white, green and red. Rating/Slope, given for each Tee, is an overall measure of the difficulty of the course, played from each respective tee.

TEE	RATING/SLOPE
GOLD	67.8/114
WHITE	65.3/106
GREEN	63.7/102
LADIES' WHITE	70.1/115
LADIES' GREEN	68.0/112
LADIES' RED	66.4/107

Scottsdale SILVERADO Golf Club

HOLE	1	2	3	4	5	6	7	8	9	Out	10	11	12	13	14	15	16	17	18	In	Tot	Hcp	Net
GOLD	514	170	441	420	303	201	401	201	525	3176	406	528	367	167	535	179	368	430	157	3137	6313		
WHITE	480	143	419	350	279	174	368	169	490	2872	376	490	342	150	506	149	333	385	131	2862	5734		
GREEN	480	143	357	350	279	157	368	150	422	2706	334	490	299	150	408	149	333	326	128	2617	5323		
RED	431	124	357	293	223	157	338	150	422	2495	334	383	299	118	408	125	280	326	128	2401	4896		
PAR	5	3	4	4	4	3	4	3	5	35	4	5	4	3	5	3	4	4	3	35	70		
MEN'S HCP	7	15	1	5	17	3	13	11	9		6	4	18	10	8	16	14	2	12				
LADIES' HCP	7	15	3	11	17	5	9	13	1		6	4	14	18	2	16	12	10	8				
DATE:		SCORER:									ATTEST:												

The top line is labelled "Hole." Note that after "9" on this line is the word "Out," and after "18 "is the word "In," followed by "Tot(al)," "Hcp," and "Net."

- "Out" is your score for the first 9 holes.
- "In" is your score for holes 10 through 18.
- "Tot" is the sum of "Out" and "In" (your **gross score**).
- "Hcp" is your **handicap**.
- "Net" is your score after your handicap is subtracted from your gross score.

The next line down, "Gold," tells golfers playing from the gold tee how long each hole is. The first hole, No. 1, is 514 yards.

The "White" line, the "Green" line and the "Red" line show the length of each hole for golfers playing from the white, green and red tees.

At the bottom of the scorecard you can see "Handicap" lines for Men and for Ladies. Look at the numbers in each of these lines. Hole handicaps rank each hole from most to least difficult.

The most difficult hole on the course for men playing from any set of tees is Hole No. 3. It is the "1" handicap hole.

The most difficult hole on the course for ladies is No. 9. See the "1?"

The **par** line tells you what the expected score for a skilled player is on each hole. Hole No. 1 is a par 5, for example. No. 2 is a par-3. Hole No. 3 is a par 4. To avoid putting pressure on yourself when you are first learning to play, don't be all that concerned with your score. Keeping score is fun as your skills improve and you begin challenging yourself to get around the course with the fewest shots possible.

The blank lines are for recording scores. Write each player's name in the boxes on the left, and enter each player's score after every hole. (Record the scores when you reach the teeing area for the next hole. This helps keep

Benchmarks –

As a new golfer, sometimes it's tough to keep an accurate score. This is especially true if you're picking up your ball and dropping it near/on the green in order to finish the hole with the rest of your group.

Even if this is the case, you can still keep score and can also set some goals for yourself by counting your putts. For example, you can note on the scorecard the number of putts you take on each hole. Another thing to count might be the number of "feel good" shots — shots that go where you intended. These can give you benchmarks on important elements of your golf game.

You might even want to record on the scorecard a smiley face ☺ for a good hole and a sad face ☹ for a hole you would have liked to play better. Try to have more smiley faces on the scorecard than sad faces!

things moving for everyone on the course, and it will minimize your chances of being hit by a ball played from the group behind you.)

At the bottom of the scorecard is a place to write the date, the name of the player who kept score, and the name of the player who checked all the addition and attested that the scores were accurate. This is important mainly when you are playing in an event that requires you to turn in your scorecard.

On the reverse side of the scorecard are the Local Rules you need to know and some other information that may be helpful — the phone number for the Golf Shop, etc.

Handicaps

The purpose of the Golf Canada Handicap and the USGA Handicap System is to make the game of golf enjoyable by enabling golfers of differing abilities to compete on an equitable basis. The handicap reflects your "potential" and not your actual average score. In Canada, to establish a Handicap Factor®, you may either belong to a golf club OR you may join your provincial golf association as a Public Players Club member. Find out more by visiting www.golfcanada.ca. In the United States, according to USGA rules, you must belong to a golf club in order to maintain a USGA Handicap Index. Most tournaments in the United States that use handicaps require that you have a USGA Handicap Index. If you want to play in one of these tournaments or if you're interested in getting a handicap index, ask someone in your local golf shop if the Club offers handicap services.

Your golf handicap index is generated by a formula based on your last 20 rounds and your ten best scores in those rounds. You can establish a handicap with as few as five 18-hole rounds, ten 9-hole rounds, or a combination of the two — so long as you play these rounds under the Rules of Golf.

Course Guides or Yardage Books

Course guides are booklets or two-sided cards that provide pictures and details for each hole. They vary in quality and level of detail from one course to another, and some courses don't offer them at all. Many courses include a diagram of each hole on the scorecard. Upscale courses give each player a booklet with either a photograph or an illustration of each hole. Distances to bunkers and penalty areas are shown, as are distances from various spots on the fairway to the green. Some guides even offer tips on how to play each hole.

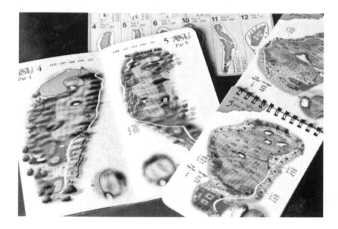

Global Positioning System (GPS) technology has a very large presence in the world of golf. More and more courses have golf carts with GPS monitors that provide you with detailed information on the placement of and distance to various features on the course. GPS monitors definitely speed up the pace of play because they provide the information you need to quickly determine which club to hit and which direction to go. Personal GPS devices or DMDs (Distance Measuring Devices) are also commonplace. Examples of DMDs include handheld GPS units, watches, range finders and SmartPhone apps.

Golf — A Sport for Life

"I've been pretty lucky to have a vocation that's also my avocation. I work in the golf industry, but golf also fills a good percentage of my free time spent with family and friends. My husband and I have been enjoying destination golf trips for the past 10 years. It's on my bucket list to play golf in all 50 states. I'm up to 28. We like to attend golf tournaments, too. I've made it to four U.S. Opens, six PGA Championships, and The Masters 10 years in a row. That's something I really like about golf—it's a sport for life that people of all ages and abilities can play and enjoy. The beauty of the USGA (United States Golf Association) handicap system is that it makes the game equal for all players. I can't walk onto a basketball court and expect to beat Michael Jordan, but I have a fair chance of winning against anyone on a golf course. I played 18 holes with the great and wonderful Nancy Lopez recently. Lost, but hey. I had a fair chance.

"People ask me all the time if I have any tips that might help them play better. I tell them to watch the pros—and not just on television. Go to tournaments. It's always a fun environment and experience, especially the Solheim Cup and Ryder Cup tournaments, which are positively electric. But more importantly, certainly for new golfers, you can observe the pros close up. Watch how they warm up and prepare to play; their pre-shot routines; how they manage the course; how they conduct themselves; how they interact with their playing partners and even the fans. I think you learn a lot just watching them, and I'll suggest that average golfers can perhaps identify more with LPGA players because of swing speed and various other mechanical aspects of hitting a golf ball. Take in an LPGA tournament if you have the chance. You might have an opportunity to shake a hand or get an autograph. The lady Tour players are very appreciative of their fans. One other reason to go to tournaments is that you can see the pros playing a course that you can play too. You can't take batting practice at Wrigley Field, but you sure can play golf on the same grass the big kids play on."

Le Ann Finger
Director of Tournaments & Player Development
Arizona Golf Association

Chapter

9

We're Up –
Let's Play Some Golf!

"Treat everyone you meet as though they're the most important person you'll meet that day."

~ Roger Dawson

On a warm and sunny day, when cotton ball clouds float lazily on the sky, the grass has been cut, every fragrant flower in the world is blooming nearby, and you're hanging with three friends — and it's a weekday — you wonder why you didn't take up golf much sooner in life.

The great thing is, you DID take it up, and now you're about to play your first round. You hear something like this:

> "Now on the number one tee, Scottsdale Silverado Golf Club welcomes the (your name) foursome. Ladies, whenever you're ready."

You and your foursome (let's name your three friends Barbara, Connie and Diane) decide to play from the Forward tees. Each of you has marked your ball with a permanent marker — a dot or a line or your initial, something that identifies it as your ball. You have decided

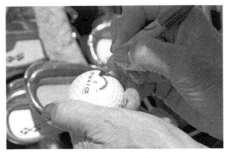

who will hit first, second, third and last. A common way to determine your hitting order is to flip a tee into the air: whoever it points to when it lands plays first, and so on. (On all holes after the first one, the player with the lowest score on the previous hole has the **honors** and hits first.)

NOTE: When players in the same group are playing from different tee markers (two players playing the Forward Tees and two players playing from the White Tees, for example) the "Back" (White) Tee plays first. Think safety!

Wouldn't you know it? The tee landed pointing at you, so you're up!

You know from looking at the Silverado scorecard that this first hole is a par 5 and 431 yards long, Forward Tee to the center of the green. You want your ball to go as far as possible on your tee shot, so you choose to hit your Driver or, if you feel more confident with it, your 3-wood. So far, so good.

You are allowed to tee up your ball using a wooden or plastic tee ONLY ON YOUR TEE SHOTS — in other words, only on the first shot for each hole that you hit from the teeing area.

two club lengths

Where to Tee Up Your Ball

Look at the teeing area. At the front of it are two red markers. You may tee up your ball anywhere behind and between those markers. You may go up to two club lengths behind them and within two club lengths of an imaginary line connecting them.

There's no need to be nervous about being first to hit — but many, many golfers confess they ARE nervous about it, so welcome to the club! Just take a deep breath, envision a beautiful shot and swing away! Watch your ball so you know where to find it.

Placing the Tee in the Ground and the Ball on the Tee

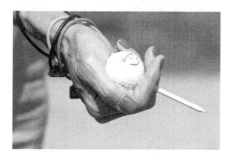

One of the easiest ways to place the tee into the ground (and look like you know what you're doing) is to start by holding the ball in the palm of your hand. At the same time, place a tee in your hand with the large round top of the tee between your index and middle fingers, and hold it so that the ball is touching the top part of the tee. Holding the ball and tee together, place the tip of the tee in the ground. Press down on the ball (and, therefore, on the tee at the same time) with your palm to get the tee into the ground at the height you want. And there you are — the ball will already be on the tee! According to Auburn University's women's golf coach, Melissa Luellen, using the pressure from your palm rather than your fingers to sink the tee into the ground will also save many a broken fingernail!

As each player tees off, the other three players remain quiet and still, out of peripheral view, and watch the flight of the ball. It is quite acceptable to compliment a player who hits a good shot.

How High to Tee Your Ball

When hitting the ball off the tee with a wood, set your club head on the ground behind the ball. The general rule of thumb is that at least half of the ball should appear above the crown of your club head. The goal is to position the ball in line with the "sweet spot" on the club. If you tee the ball too high, then when you swing, the club might go underneath the ball, popping it high into the air and advancing it far less than you anticipated. When hitting the ball with an iron, tee the ball up only slightly so that it looks inviting to hit.

Hitting a Provisional Ball

"Special" shots happen!

When a player hits a shot that appears to go out of bounds or may not be findable, she should hit a **provisional ball** from the same spot. Let's imagine that Barbara hooks her tee shot into the desert area along the left side of the fairway. White stakes mark the out-of-bounds line.

It appears that her ball might be **OB**, but Barbara is not sure. There is always the chance that the ball hit a rock or something and bounced back into the fairway. It would be safely in play in this case. But since Barbara is unsure whether the ball is in or out of bounds, she must declare (say aloud) that she is hitting a provisional ball. If her first ball is OB, she will play her provisional ball (assuming that the provisional ball is in bounds). Your foursome can now proceed to your next shots.

NOTE: Hitting the provisional ball when in doubt helps maintain your pace of play. There is nothing that hurts pace of play (and your pride!) more than having to go all the way back to the tee (where another group may be waiting!) to hit another ball after you discover that your first ball is lost or OB.

After hitting your tee shot, be sure to pick up your wooden or plastic tee for reuse. If it is broken, pick up the pieces and discard them in the designated container or, if one is not present, leave them next to the tee marker.

*Some golf courses provide a bucket of divot/seed mixture on the teeing area so players can fill in their **divots**. There is usually a container of this material with each golf cart, too, so you can fill in fairway divots. And no, these containers are not for cigarette butts.*

High fives all around, ladies! You're off!

A Gracious Lesson

"I started playing golf with my husband for fun. We would play late in the summer day — a few bucks for as many holes as you could finish before sundown (that was about the right price for how I played then).

"Years later, I started playing regularly with women and learned that the fun, good company, scenery and fresh air were more important than the score. I enjoyed tournament play where I felt pressure to play well, and was also happy to play for fun with a group that just picked up their bad shots. I realize the latter is not really playing golf, but it is enjoying friends and colleagues on the golf course, which in some cases is just perfect. It is crucial, however, to know the difference and to follow the customs and etiquette of golf when appropriate.

"I learned a lesson in graciousness from a scratch golfer in my business foursome when he announced on the first tee that, because this was not the US Open, he hoped no one would mind if he had a horrible shot, he picked up his ball or tossed it into the fairway. Of course, he was not going to have ANY bad shots, but we all were relaxed and had more fun because he (the best golfer of us) set the tone that this was for fun. We ended up sticking pretty close to the Rules anyway, but it was very gracious on his part. When the day comes that I am by far the best golfer in my foursome, I hope I will be that gracious myself (and even before then, in smaller ways).

"Currently, I love to head out for a game of 9 or 18 holes with my clients, colleagues, friends and even my daughters! I have deepened relationships and friendships in a relaxed environment. And it's true — you really do learn a lot about people by playing golf with them."

Robyn Nordin Stowell
Golf and Private Club Attorney with National Practice

10

Welcome to
Your First Fairway!

"The potential of the average person is like a huge
ocean unsailed, a new continent unexplored,
a world of possibilities waiting to be released and
channeled toward some great good."

~ Brian Tracy

For the sake of simplicity, let's assume Barbara is your cart partner.
You drive to the spot where you last saw her ball and stop to look
for the ball in the desert. Always take a golf club with you when you
are looking for a ball, so you can retrieve the ball if it is under a bush
or hard to reach.

After a couple of minutes of looking, you find that Barbara's ball is
indeed out of bounds. You then go either to her provisional ball or
your ball, whichever one is FARTHEST FROM THE GREEN. In golf,
the player who is farthest from the target (the hole marked with the
flag on the green) hits first.

Your tee shot went farther than Barbara's provisional ball, so she will
hit before you play your second shot.

Because her first ball could not be found, Barbara is playing her
provisional ball, and she now "lies 3." Here's why: her first stroke

was the shot off the tee, her second stroke was actually a penalty stroke and when she hit the provisional ball it was her third stroke. The next ball she hits will be her fourth stroke. After Barbara hits, you proceed to your ball and assess your situation. Well done — your ball is in the middle of the fairway!

First, look at the ball without touching it to confirm it is your ball. You "lie 1." The next ball you hit will be your second stroke. But how far is it to the green? Which club should you hit? You need to determine where you are, but how?

Ready Golf—

Ready golf helps maintain a proper pace of play. Normally the player farthest from the hole hits first, but in ready golf, it's whoever is ready to hit. You can play ready golf off the tee, in the fairway or around the green. Just make sure that your playing partners have agreed to play ready golf and aren't in danger of being hit by your ball.

Every golf course provides key distance markers to help you calculate which club to use for each shot. Most fairways are marked in the middle with indicators at the 100-yard distance, the 150-yard distance, the 200-yard distance and, on longer holes, the 250-yard distance. Also, these same distances may be marked on the cart paths. To determine your distance from one of these markers, pace it off. For a person of average height, a slightly longer than normal step is about one yard.

Sprinkler heads can often help you too. Find a nearby sprinkler head. There is a number on it. Let's say you find one right by your ball and the number on it is "281." Here's what you now know:

You are about 280 yards from the center of the green. (Nice drive — you hit it about 150 yards!)

This is a par 5 hole, so ideally you'd like to be on the green with your third shot. This would

150 yard pole

281 yard marker

fairway bunker

put you on the green **in regulation**, i.e., in position to make a one-putt **birdie** or a two-putt par.

About 130 yards ahead, there is a very large fairway bunker on the right side of the fairway. How do you know it is 130 yards to the bunker?

> In the middle of the fairway ahead of you is a black and white pole. This pole is 150 yards from the center of the green. The sand bunker is approximately even with the pole. Voila! — 280 minus 150 is 130.

To get safely past the bunker you need to hit your second shot 140 yards, which may be pushing it at this stage of your skill development. You

What color is the flag on the green?

Most golf courses use the American Golf red/white/blue system. A red flag means the hole is in the front third of the green; a white flag indicates the hole is in the middle of the green; and a blue flag indicates the hole is in the back third of the green. Depending on flag color, you might need to add or subtract 5 – 10 yards when calculating how far you want to hit your approach shot. Similarly, in the fairway, you might see a red indicator for the 100-yard distance, a white indicator for the 150-yard distance, and a blue indicator for the 200-yard distance.

should keep this in mind when making your club selection, and aim to hit your ball to the middle of the fairway (away from the bunker). If you do this, you will "take the bunker out of play."

Then you will be ready for your third shot, with the goal being to hit your ball onto the green in regulation.

Envision your shot each time, take a practice swing and then swing away!

The four of you continue to advance to the green, taking turns according to whose ball is farthest from the target, which today is marked with a red flag.

As you get closer, notice the "Carts" signs in the fairway. The arrows on these signs direct you to the cart path, as you are not allowed to drive your cart on the fairway as you approach the green. If a player's ball is sitting between

Extra Clubs Help Pace of Play –

*On occasion, a golf course will ask you to keep the carts on the cart paths for the entire round. To help maintain a good pace of play when you have to walk to your ball and aren't sure what kind of lie you have or how far you will need to hit, **bracket** your club selection. For example, if you think you will need a 7-iron, take your 8-iron and your 6-iron, too. That way you have it covered. You may also want to take your putter so you can walk straight to the green without having to come back to the cart.*

these markers and the green, it may make sense for the player to grab her putter and a few clubs and walk the rest of the way to her ball and then to the green. If she does this, make sure the other player takes the cart to the green-side cart path. If, after you putt, you have to run back and retrieve the cart, it will slow the pace of play.

If the Guys Can Do It, So Can We

"My boss said I had to play in the 'Fresh Start' golf tournament because our company was an Elite level sponsor. I quickly took a lesson at Phoenix Country Club beforehand so that I'd know how to hold the handle. But the reason we Wells Fargo women started playing regularly is because we saw all the guys leaving during the day to play golf — and the bank was sponsoring their participation. Duh!

"Aside from simply doing something that is fun, I found that golf was good for my business relationships — either to thank customers or to obtain new ones."

Edythe L. Higgins
Business Banker – retired

Get a Game

"Do I wish I could play better? Of course. When people ask how my golf game is I say, 'Well, it's mine.' Having a golf game is what is important. Not how you play, nor how often, nor with whom. Just have a golf game. It does wonders for your social life and business life alike. Or at least it can, if you let it. Have I made mistakes in business? None that a mulligan wouldn't have fixed."

Kate Rakoci
CEO and Founder
Jack Of All Trades

The Green and Your Short Game

"Never let the fear of striking out get in your way."

~ *George Herman "Babe" Ruth*

The green is truly happy land, the place every player is trying to get to. It's the big target that surrounds the bulls-eye — the hole marked by a red, white or blue flag. If you reach the green in regulation, you've hit some great shots to get there — and on occasion, lucky shots, too! When you aren't quite on the green in regulation, the most important part of your golf game comes into play — your short game.

The short game is a term golfers use when they're referring to **chipping**, **pitching** and **putting**. These are the kinds of shots you'll be using around and on the green. To help explain this part of the game, imagine that this is the situation when your foursome reaches the green:

> You've hit three tremendous shots and find your ball sitting on the green approximately 20 feet past the hole. (Way to go!)

Barbara's ball is in the greenside bunker on the left side of the green.

Connie finds her ball on fluffy grass, to the right of the green, but there is a greenside bunker between her ball and the green.

Diane's ball is nestled on a grassy mound just beyond the back of the green.

Who plays first? Diane is farthest from the hole, so she plays first. Before she plays, however, you should mark your ball's location with a coin or marker. After you mark your ball, move to the side of the green, out of her path and line of vision.

Diane uses a wedge to execute a little chip shot. A chip is like a putt but with a low-flying start. Her goal is to get the ball out of the grass and rolling on the green toward the hole. Diane's ball stops just short of your ball marker. She marks her ball with a ball marker before the next player plays.

Connie is farther from the hole than Barbara, so she hits next. She will have to execute a pitch shot up and over the bunker using a high-lofted club such as her pitching wedge, sand wedge or lob wedge. If she does this properly, her ball will land softly and safely on the green. She succeeds and her ball stops within a few feet of the flagstick in the hole, also called the "flag" or "pin." (Great shot, Connie!)

Barbara is the only player not yet on the green. She enters the bunker, taking a rake with her (to help keep the pace of play moving). She manages to get her ball out of the sand and onto the green using a sand wedge, but the ball rolls across the green and into the grass on the other side.

*NOTE: **Playing your ball out of a Bunker** – Prior to hitting your shot, you can remove any **loose impediments** as long as in doing so you won't move your ball. This includes natural objects like a twig, a pinecone or a leaf. You can also remove **movable obstructions**, which are artificial things like a paper cup or a candy wrapper.*

Mark Your Ball on the Green –

Mark your ball on the green so your playing partners have a clear view of their putts. The green is the only place on the golf course where you can mark your ball. You may use anything for a marker — a lucky coin, the removable

marker that comes on some golf gloves, or a plastic disk. The over-whelming majority of players put the marker behind the ball, and you should, too, but you can put it on either side or in front of the ball. Just be consistent about it because you'll incur a penalty if you fail to put your ball back EXACTLY WHERE IT WAS. Also, if your marker is in another player's putting line and she asks you to move it left or right, move your marker the length of one putter head in this way:

1. Set the heel of your putter on the green, right next to your marker.

2. Position your putter head so that it points to a stationary object, such as a tree.

3. Move your marker the length of one putter head — NOT the length of your putter. If you place your marker upside down at the end of the putter head, it will remind you that you will need to move it back before you can putt.

Be sure to reverse this procedure exactly to re-position your marker when it is your turn to putt.

You are allowed to place any extra clubs you might have with you onto the sand inside the bunker. However, you are NOT allowed to ground your club onto the sand either in front of or behind your ball prior to taking your stroke. After hitting your ball out of the bunker, rake the sand so that there is no evidence you were there, i.e., leave it smooth.

After Barbara rakes the bunker to erase her tracks, she can play her next shot. While you are waiting for her to get to her ball, repair any ball marks you see, especially any that your ball might have made when it landed on the green.

When Barbara is ready to play, she elects to use her putter even though her ball is not on the green. Because it isn't on the green, she might choose to keep the flagstick in the hole or have it pulled out. Many players in this situation prefer to keep the flagstick in, because if they hit the ball too firmly but on the right line, the flagstick will stop the ball from rolling too far past the hole. All players whose golf balls are on the green have the same choice of whether they would like to have the flagstick pulled out of the hole. There is no penalty for hitting the flagstick when putting your ball on the green.

Barbara's ball stops about six feet from the hole.

The group chooses to have the flag removed from the hole when putting. Connie is closest to the hole, so she **tends the flag**. (Before pulling out the flagstick, she asks whether everyone can see the hole.) Diane putts first because she is farthest away.

How to Tend the Flag

- Give it a little twist as you're pulling it out, which makes it easier. Be careful to avoid hitting the edge of the hole when you remove the flagstick and when you put it back in.

- Place the flagstick on the ground away from where any player will be putting so that it isn't a distraction and can't be hit by an errant putt.

- Always lay the flagstick on the green gently — tossing it or dropping it could dent the putting surface or damage the grass.

- Generally, the player who holes out first (i.e., gets her ball in the hole) takes responsibility for replacing the flagstick in the hole once all of the players in the group have finished. If it's easier for someone else to do it, no problem, especially if it helps the pace of play.

3 Steps to Reading the Green

Greens typically have some slope or undulation, which allows the water to drain properly and helps the golf course architect give golfers a little extra challenge. Being a good putter requires understanding how the ball will curve, slow down, or speed up as it heads to the hole. Sometimes it might curve in both directions, or go up and down more than once.

1. As you approach the green from the fairway or cart path, take advantage of the opportunity to view the topography of the green and how it might affect the path of your ball once you hit it toward the hole. How is the green sloped?

2. When you're standing behind your ball, ask yourself, "If I poured a glass of water onto the green, which way would the water run?" If you're putting uphill, the ball will travel more slowly and have less **break** than if you are putting downhill. Remember, the law of gravity prevails!

3. It's helpful to pay attention when your playing partners attempt their putts. Notice the direction and speed the balls travel, especially when they are close to the hole.

Courtesy Around the Green

Even for skilled players, putting can be intense — after all, a 2-foot putt counts the same as a 250-yard drive! Because of this, play around the green requires specific etiquette. Some of the key aspects are:

Heed the "Sacred Ground:" There's an imaginary line between another player's ball and the hole. NEVER STEP ON THIS LINE! It's best to walk around the outside of your playing

partner's ball or ball marker so you don't step on the imaginary line. If you're sure you're not going to violate the space, you may step gingerly over it. There's no penalty for stepping on someone's line, but it makes you look inconsiderate and ignorant, and it certainly doesn't endear you to your playing partners.

"sacred ground"

Where to Stand: The imaginary line also has implications for where you should stand while waiting your turn. You shouldn't stand in any other player's line. This includes the line that extends behind her and directly across from her on the other side of the hole.

Know Your Shadow: You don't want your shadow to cross anyone's line, so be sure to keep yourself positioned appropriately. This is especially noteworthy early and late in the day when shadows can be quite long.

Putting Order Options: If your ball is farthest from the hole, you are considered to be **away** or **out**. You would putt first. If you don't make your putt, you may ask your playing partners if they'd mind if you finish. This is one way of maintaining your group's pace of play. There are a few reasons you may choose NOT to continue:

How to Repair a Ball Mark

*Ball marks (you might also hear them referred to as **pitch marks**) are indentations caused when a ball lands on the green. Unrepaired ball marks can take two to three weeks to properly heal, leaving behind an unsightly and uneven putting surface. A repaired ball mark takes less than half that time to heal.*

As a steward of the game, fix your ball mark and any others you see while your partners are putting. The rule of thumb is to fix your mark and one other.

There's really not much to it:

- *Use a divot repair tool or a tee;*

- *Insert it at the edges of the ball mark — not the middle of the depression;*

- *Bring the edges together with a gentle twisting motion, but don't lift the center — you don't want to tear the roots;*

- *Gently tap the surface with the bottom of your putter or your foot;*

You're done when it's a surface you would want to putt over.

- You'd be standing in another player's line.
- You want time to line up your next putt.
- You want to "regroup" from a "special" putt and need time to refocus.

If this is the case, mark your ball and be ready to play your shot promptly when it's time.

Before You Leave the Green

Check to make sure your foursome has picked up all the clubs that were brought to the green. One good way to avoid leaving clubs behind is to place any extra clubs next to the flagstick if it is pulled. Or, leave them at the edge of the green where you will see them easily on your way back to the golf carts.

I Don't Talk Business During Client Golf

"I hired a life coach whose background was in sports psychology. During one of our sessions he asked whether I played golf. I'd hit a few balls before, but that's about it. So he said we should have a session at a golf course, because it would be fun and it's a great place to get to know someone. He said, in a round of golf, everyone becomes who they are, that it all comes out. We went and I hit a few good shots along with the bad shots. He helped me believe I could do it, and I stuck with it.

"A major source of business for me is referrals, so I tend to golf a lot with business colleagues, more so than with clients. I don't like to talk business when I am golfing with a client, but I DO talk business when golfing with colleagues. We have some common ground. Sometimes I can help them with a client need, and sometimes they can help me. There's a lot of cross-promotion.

"I try to play in at least one charity golf event per month. It's fun, and it's an opportunity to give something back to the community."

Lana Hock
Senior Vice President
The Hock Group
Robert W. Baird & Co.

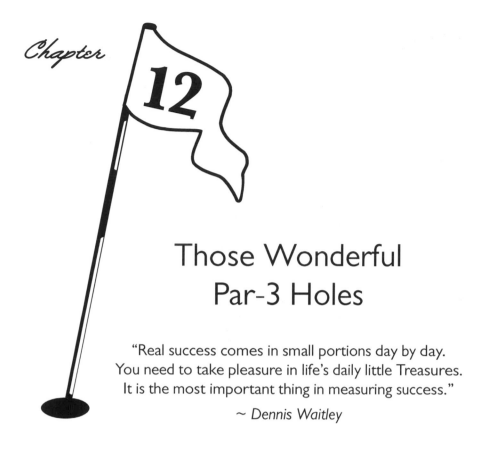

Chapter

12

Those Wonderful
Par-3 Holes

"Real success comes in small portions day by day.
You need to take pleasure in life's daily little Treasures.
It is the most important thing in measuring success."

~ Dennis Waitley

Most golfers welcome the opportunity to play a par-3 hole during their rounds because par-3s are shorter holes and are reachable in one shot. Most championship-length par 72 courses have four par-3s. But what par-3s lack in distance they make up for in difficulty.

At Scottsdale Silverado Golf Course, the second hole is a 124-yard par-3 from the Forward Tee. As you stand on the tee contemplating which club to use, note the color and location of the flag. Also observe that the green is slightly higher in elevation than the teeing area that you're standing on, there is a greenside bunker located at the left front of the green, and there is a backstop mound at the back of the green.

The flag is red, and you know that means the hole is located in the front third of the green. The flag is also on the left side of the green, which brings the greenside bunker into play. If your shot is short, there is a very good chance you'll end up in the bunker. This hole location is often called a "sucker pin" because, even though the shorter distance initially makes the hole seem easy, a bunker lies in waiting.

Because the green is elevated slightly, add 5-10 yards to the distance. However, because the flag is red, you'll want to subtract about 10 yards from the distance shown on the scorecard. After you do the math in your head, you determine that you need to choose a club that will send your ball about 120 yards.

Which club do you hit? First, think of which club you use for a shot of 100 yards: your 7-iron. This means your 6-iron should give you a shot of 110 yards or so, and your 5-iron — Voila! — a shot of 120 yards. There is no need to worry about hitting it too long, because there is the mound in the back. The safe play is to aim for the center of the green, because you'll be about the right distance AND you will take the greenside bunker out of play.

After each player hits her tee shot you proceed to the green. Connie has unfortunately hit her ball far to the left. This is about when you notice the "Cart Path Only" or "Keep Carts on Path" signs. Connie must walk to her ball.

Uncertain what kind of lie she has, she takes two or three clubs with her, including her putter. There are a couple reasons for taking several clubs when you have to walk across the fairway to reach your ball:

- When you reach your ball, you want to be sure you have the right club so that you don't have to return to the cart before hitting.

- You don't know what kind of lie you have. Is it in deep grass or a divot, or is it okay? Also, what if you hit your shot poorly and your ball lands in the greenside bunker? You may need an additional club for that.

Par-3 holes offer the potential for a **hole-in-one**, arguably the biggest thrill a golfer can experience. But keep in mind that making par on a par-3 is a great score (making par on any hole is a great score!), so playing it safe by aiming for the middle of the green is always a good option.

When to Say "Uncle" and Pick Up

When you are on an airplane flying somewhere and you hear the pilot making an announcement, you listen. So listen to this announcement from Delta Airlines Captain Kim Hinshaw, who, when she isn't flying, is playing golf:

"When I am playing a casual round of golf with friends, my personal rule is to pick up my ball as soon as it becomes obvious that the best I can do is make double par or more on the hole. If I muff a couple shots, for example, I might ask the long driver in the group if she would mind me dropping my ball where hers lies and playing the rest of the hole from there. Or, I might just drop my ball on the green when the other players in my group have reached the green. I'll putt out for the practice.

"Golf is a game meant to be fun and entertaining, particularly when you're starting out, so do whatever it takes to keep your smile intact. Say 'Uncle' and pick up. You're in a beautiful setting with leisure time to be there. Enjoy every minute and start over on the next hole."

Does Anyone Here Play Golf?

"I am pretty new to golf, but already there are some things I can tell you. One, the more I play, the more often I hit good shots, and the more SAWEET shots I hit, the more self-confidence I have on and off the course. Two, relationships I'm developing through golf (player to ball, player to players, player to self) are shedding light on instinctive reactions I have to certain traits of mine — letting go of the negativity I feel when I hit a poor shot allows me to enjoy the entire round, for example. Three, being perceived as *a golfer* gives me a little boost of confidence. Four, when I am with a bunch of people I don't know, I have discovered a great way to say I am engaging and approachable: I ask, 'Does anyone else here play golf?'"

Amy Waitkus
Sales & Marketing Coordinator
Video West

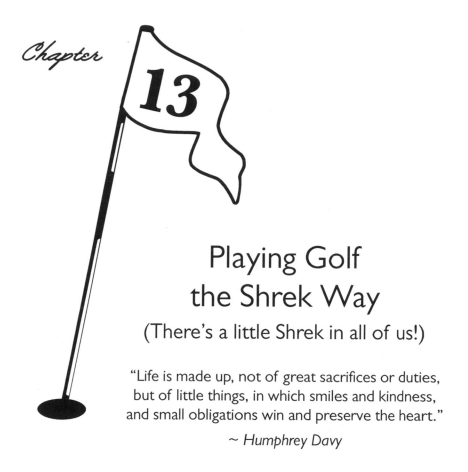

Chapter 13

Playing Golf
the Shrek Way

(There's a little Shrek in all of us!)

"Life is made up, not of great sacrifices or duties,
but of little things, in which smiles and kindness,
and small obligations win and preserve the heart."

~ *Humphrey Davy*

An awkward aspect of taking up golf later in life is that you look like an adult, and aren't adults supposed to look like they know what they are doing? But, like Tom Hanks' character in *Big*, the reality is that on the golf course, you're a little kid in a grownup's body — until you do know what you are doing.

My son Ben and I discovered our *SHREK* when Ben was taking golf lessons as a youngster. One of the things the instructor wanted his students to learn was golf etiquette. He told them there would be a test. Seeing that Ben was struggling to remember everything, I sat down with him and together we came up a mnemonic device. (The irony of taking etiquette advice from an ogre! But it sure made it all memorable for a 10-year-old boy.)

Here's what we put together, modified a bit for an adult audience:

S = Watch out for the *Safety* of others

- Before you take a practice swing or a real swing, look around and make sure no one is close to you.
- Don't hit your ball if there's a chance you might hit someone in your group or in the group ahead of you — golf balls don't always go where you want them to, particularly when you're starting out.
- If you think your ball is going to hit someone, yell "Fore!" immediately and loudly.

H = *Help* your partners and other golfers

- If someone forgets a golf club on the ground, pick it up and hand it to her.
- Watch where your partner's ball goes, and help her search for it if it doesn't land in the fairway.
- Repair your divots in the fairway, fix your ball marks on the green and smooth the sand in the bunkers.

R = *Really* forgive others

- If someone makes a noise, talks, or distracts you while you're hitting, don't blame them for your poor shot. Move on to the next one.
- If you're playing a game and a partner lets you down with a bad shot, she's probably already feeling bad. Support her.

E = *Express* gratitude

- Shake hands with your playing partners at the end of your round, thanking them for their company.
- If you're a guest, you can express your gratitude by picking up the first round of beverages on the course, or the first round after golf when you are in the clubhouse — also known as the **19th hole**.

K = *Kindness* is king

- Yes, golf can be frustrating, but watch your language.
- Competition is part of the game, but it takes a back seat to fair play and sportsmanship.

As you can see from the acronym, golf is valuable for building character and teaching life skills to children (and to adults!). Ben did pass his test, by the way.

"Would You Like To Play Through?"

When you are part of a foursome and the group behind you is a twosome, occasionally they have to wait on you. Knowing that someone is waiting on you can feel very uncomfortable. Ask them if they would like to play through or just wave them through. They might even ask you if you'd mind, and that's fine.

If you offer them the opportunity to play through and they accept, move to the side of the fairway or an appropriate location so that you are not in danger of being hit by one of their golf balls.

They will (should!) thank you as they pass by. Wish them a good round and resume playing once they are out of range.

Be mindful that maintaining a good pace of play means that you keep up with the group ahead. So, if you are being pressed by the group behind you, make sure it's because your foursome is waiting on the group ahead of you, not because your foursome is playing slowly. Always focus forward, not back.

Oh No! A Woman! And Then I Hit It

"Golf wasn't an instant attraction for me. I had a hard time understanding why people would pay so much for a frustrating experience. Besides, I could throw the ball farther than I could hit it. But, one day, I hit a really good shot and thought, *Oh! THAT'S why you do it!* I didn't play that often until I moved from Green Bay to Chicago and didn't know anyone. Golf became a focal point because it let me meet people. I could hit it and was comfortable calling up and asking for a tee time for a single. I'd always get put with three men. Their shoulders would slump and I knew they were thinking, *Oh, no. A woman!* And then I'd outdrive them. By the second hole we'd be exchanging business cards."

Char Carson
LPGA Professional

Unintended Consequences

"I grew up playing competitive tennis. Friends played golf, but it just wasn't my thing. Then, when I began making my own way in the business world, colleague peer pressure compelled me to try it. I wasn't a fan. I remained skeptical. Eventually I made the decision to give it a go and took a 30-minute lesson. I'm Type A all the way. Losing isn't in my vocabulary. I have to win. I was going to be the best Amateur golfer I could be, and knew I'd be spending hours upon hours at the driving range hitting golf balls. After I took my first lesson I went to the Scottsdale Cigar Club, where I was a member. They were raffling off a set of Adams golf clubs, so I bought a ticket. And won. My quest for perfection was off and running—and I would soon learn more about myself than I would ever have known without golf.

"One Sunday afternoon I took two coworkers to a Golf for Cause Nine & Wine golf mentoring outing. I'd found these to be a great introduction to golf. Debbie was our assigned mentor and asked each of us to pick one goal for the day. I wanted to work on having a consistent pre-shot routine. After displaying frustration over one of my shots on just our second hole, Debbie pulled me aside and suggested I change my goal. My self-absorption and negativity on the course could easily translate into a perception of how I show up in the workplace. PLUS, I risked being welcomed as a playing partner in future outings. Debbie encouraged me to stop berating myself and instead to say something positive about every shot I took. Back at the office, I mentioned my learning experience to a peer with whom I'd played golf several times. "Portland, now you know why I don't play with you anymore." Wow!

"The next time I played golf, I was paired with another single. I said something good about every shot under my breath. At the end of the round he shook my hand and said, "You're the most positive person I've ever played with!"

"It took golf to teach me that winning at any cost is not fine. I went from hitting 400-600 balls a day to losing friends and hurting some of my business relationships. People didn't want to play with me. Thank you, Debbie Waitkus, for opening my eyes to things I needed to see. Golf has made me a better person. A better friend. A better daughter. A better businessperson. Golf can be a humbling game, and it crushed me, but it put me back together in a way I couldn't have imagined. Am I fun to play golf with? I am NOW!"

Portland Reed
Forever grateful to the game

These Things Happen

"Small improvements in the way you use your time can translate into major differences in your life."

~ *Brian Tracy*

Golf is a fun game governed by Rules of play every player is expected to know. There really aren't that many rules, despite the common perception to the contrary. But golf is renowned for the honesty and sportsmanship that players embrace and expect of one another. Golf is a game of integrity, and golfers are obligated to call penalties on themselves.

If you find yourself wondering whether you can legally do something on the golf course and suspect there is a rule about it, check the Golf Canada and/or USGA (United States Golf Association) Rules of Golf book that you carry in your golf bag. (Yes! Buy one and keep it in your bag. You don't need to read it cover to cover, but keep it handy as a reference tool.) You can also download the USGA Rules of Golf App onto your Smart Phone. If you are playing in a tournament, ask a tournament official. When playing a casual round of golf with friends, consult your fellow players.

In addition to normal, everyday situations, the Rules of Golf cover all sorts of oddball circumstances, from what happens if an animal steals your ball off the fairway (you replace a ball where it was, no penalty) to what you do if the wind is blowing so hard that it moves your ball when it was previously sitting still in the fairway (no penalty, simply hit it from the new spot).

When you are learning to play golf, the rules can seem so intimidating they become distracting. While it is true that knowledge is power (and ignorance is bliss!), knowing every rule is not critically important when you are enjoying a round of casual, less structured golf. Recall that my first experience on a golf course included learning how to play a foot wedge!

The USGA.org website offers practice quizzes where you can test your knowledge of the Rules. Build your confidence and see how you do!

Once you gain more experience, the Rules make more and more sense. Here are some of the most common things beginning golfers ask about and the rules that apply to them, including some changes to the Rules effective January 2019. Oh, and to make things easier to understand — because the official rules of golf are technical and dry — they are demystified with simpler language here:

What Happens if My Ball Falls Off the Tee?

- **Rule 6.2 (5) Ball Falling Off Tee**

  If you didn't intend to hit the ball to put it into play, you can re-tee your ball without penalty. Note that IF YOU SWING AT THE BALL AND WHIFF, IT COUNTS AS A STROKE. If you barely touch the ball or the wind from your whiff blows the ball off the tee, you need to hit your next shot (counting it as your second shot) from where it lies — no re-teeing the ball.

What Do I Do if I Lose My Ball or Hit It Out of Bounds?

You read about this situation in Chapter 9 when Barbara hit the provisional ball. Just remember that, whether you hit the ball out of bounds or the ball is declared lost, you'll follow the same steps to get your ball back into play.

- **Rule 18-2a When a Ball Is Lost or Out of Bounds**

    The Rules of Golf allow you to look for your ball for up to three minutes before declaring it "lost." Remember that three minutes seems like an eternity when you are on the golf course, and it is, in terms of pace of play.

    Captain Kim Hinshaw (see Chapter 12, *When to Say "Uncle" and Pick Up*) offers this excellent advice about lost balls: "I have a 30-second rule on finding a lost ball. Some balls are just meant to be short-term relationships. A buck or two a ball is not worth taking time away from the other players or getting a rattlesnake bite — rumored to cost up to $75K in medical expenses. Just let it go."

What Do I Do if My Ball Is on the Cart Path?

- **16.1 Abnormal Course Conditions (Including Immovable Obstructions)**

    Golf balls occasionally land on the cart path. The cart path is an example of an "abnormal course condition" or an "immovable obstruction." You get free relief (no penalty) when your ball is on a cart path or other immovable obstruction like a sprinkler head. This also applies when your ball is close enough to an immovable obstruction to affect your stance or your swing if you tried to hit it.

- In most instances, you pick up the ball and drop it from knee height within one club-length of your nearest point of relief (the point where you can take a clear swing at the ball). You cannot drop the ball any closer to the hole, and there is no penalty.

- ## 15.2 Movable Obstructions

  There are also such things as moveable obstructions. Common moveable obstructions include a rake, a cart path sign, or another player's club, for example. Simply move the obstruction.

  If your ball moves during this process, return it to its original spot and continue to play. There is no penalty.

What If I Hit My Ball into Water?

- ## Rule 17-1 Relief from Ball in Penalty Area

  There are two types of penalty areas: yellow-staked penalty areas and red-staked (lateral) penalty areas. Yellow-staked penalty areas are situated such that you definitely need to hit your ball over them in order to complete the hole. Red-staked penalty areas are usually found alongside the fairway — ideally, you can play the hole without having to hit over them. Depending on which kind of penalty area your ball lands in, you have different options.

  In a yellow-staked penalty area, you have three options:

  - Play the ball from where it lies without being assessed a penalty stroke. You are allowed to ground your club in the penalty area.

yellow penalty area marker

— Take a one-stroke penalty. Now imagine a line that passes through both the hole and the spot where your ball entered the penalty area (not where your ball ended up). Drop your ball anywhere on that line behind the spot where your ball went into the penalty area. You can go back as far as you want, but you can't drop your ball closer to the hole.

— Take a one-stroke penalty, drop a ball from knee height and play your next shot from the spot where you previously hit.

Bonus option: Sometimes a par-3 hole with a yellow-staked hazard will offer a drop area close to the green. Take the one-stroke penalty, drop a ball in the drop area and carry on.

When your ball is in a red-staked penalty area, and there is no drop area, you have all the options of the yellow-staked penalty area plus two more:

— Drop your ball from knee height within two club lengths of the spot where it crossed into the penalty area, but no closer to the hole. You can use any club in your bag to determine a club length, except your putter.

red hazard markers

— Drop your ball knee height within two club lengths of the spot where it crossed into the penalty area, only on the opposite side of the penalty area. Do not drop your ball any closer to the hole.

NOTE: *You can always choose to hit your ball from within the penalty area and, thus, not incur a penalty. (Just make sure your playing partners aren't planning to make you infamous on YouTube.)*

What If My Ball Hits the Golf Cart?

- **Rule 11.1a - Ball in Motion Accidentally Hits Person or Outside Influence**

  Occasionally the ball doesn't go exactly where you visualize it going. Should it accidentally hit a golf club laying on the ground, the golf cart, another player or even yourself, not to worry. Given that you didn't intend for the mishap, no penalty is assessed to any players.

How Many Clubs Can I Carry in My Bag?

- **Rule 4-1b – Maximum of Fourteen Clubs**

  Count the clubs in your bag prior to your round. You may not have more than 14 clubs in your bag without incurring a penalty.

Who Hits First / Who Has "Honors?"

- **Rule 6.4 Order of Play When Playing Hole**
- **Rule 6.4b(1) Stroke Play Normal Order of Play, the player with the lowest score hits first on the next hole.**

  After the first shot, the player whose ball is farthest away from the hole hits first. This is also the case around the green, regardless of whether or not all the balls are on the green. The Rule still stands: whoever is farthest from the hole has honors.

  Interestingly, if a competitor plays out of turn, no penalty is incurred and the ball is played as it lies. However, a player in the group can ask the player who hit out of turn to re-hit. This once happened in a **Solheim Cup** match. Annika Sorenstam of the European team chipped the ball into the hole from off the green only to learn she was not the farthest from the cup. The Americans made her re-hit the shot. She did not replicate the chip-in.

- ## Rule 6.4b (2) Playing Out of Turn in a Safe and Responsible Way ("Ready Golf")

Whether on the first shot or shots after the tee shot, players are allowed and encouraged to play out of turn in a safe and responsible way, which can save a lot of time and promote good pace of play. You'll experience "Ready Golf" in most business and casual golf outings.

Fear Not

"I volunteer to mentor new golfers occasionally. Most of the participants are women. Working with them is enjoyable, because they are excited about learning to play. Some want to be able to play with their spouse. My wife, Susan, took it up for this reason when we were vacationing at Hilton Head years ago. We've been having ball playing together ever since. Others are getting into golf because it is a great business tool. Initially some are nervous. I tell them not to worry. The objective is to have fun. We chat briefly at the outset to loosen up and establish some goals, then play 6 or 7 holes. When someone hits a good shot it's a moment of excitement and high fives for the whole group. After that the quest is on to hit the next one. New golfers worry needlessly about slowing everyone down. I've never known any golfer who has a problem with a playing partner picking up a ball and moving forward with it to maintain pace of play. Nobody expects you to be a great or even good golfer, just a golfer. Trust that you are an equal and enjoy the game."

Jim Hall
Head of Construction/Senior Designer
Sonoran Landesign

The Games We Play

"Most people are paralyzed by fear.
Overcome it and you take charge of your life
and your world."

~ Mark Victor Hansen

One of the great things about golf is that the game is flexible, i.e., it can be played in various formats. Beginning golfers, for example, can play in **scramble** format tournaments without the pressure of having to play their own ball on every shot. Every tournament has a designated format, but when you are just out playing with friends, it can be fun to experiment with the basic formats.

When you are invited to play in a charity tournament or business-related tournament, the format will likely be a **scramble, best ball** or **modified scramble**. The scramble format is very often the first experience beginning golfers have with charitable and business-related golf outings.

The scramble format can be wildly exciting because each team player hits a tee shot on every hole, and then the players decide which ball is their best shot. When they determine which ball location is best, each player plays from that spot. The same thing follows for each shot, including the ones on the putting green, until the team holes out. This format encourages fun and camaraderie, and produces birdies and even **eagles**. Many great and lasting friendships have been born during scrambles.

Scramble format tournaments are ideal for groups that include male and female players of all skill levels, because every player has a chance to contribute to the team's success. Perhaps the only thing you do well is putt. That's great! Even if you don't putt well, you can putt first to give your teammates a chance to see the line — and every now and then the hole gets in the way and you are hailed as the hero. Any time you have a chance to participate in a scramble, do it! You'll be glad you did.

Best ball is a popular format that is often confused with the scramble format. Best ball means each player on a team plays her own ball all the way from tee to green. The team's score is the lowest (the best) score of any of the team's players for each hole.

Modified scramble, also called a **shamble** or Texas scramble, is a combination of the best ball and scramble formats. Each player tees off and the team selects the best shot; then, everyone plays her own ball from that spot the rest of the way to the hole. The team score is the lowest (the best) score made by any of the team's players.

What is a shotgun start? In order for a large group of players to start and finish at the same time, foursomes start off simultaneously on different holes of the golf course. In an earlier time, golf tournaments were often started, literally, with the blast of a shotgun, which could be heard from anywhere on the golf course.

The only potentially confusing thing about a shotgun start is the way you will need to write down your team's score after your first hole. It's likely that your team started on, say, the 7th hole. Out of habit, golfers enter their first hole score in the No. 1 hole column, but in this case, it should be entered in the No. 7 column. The final hole for this team would be the 6th hole.

Many charity tournaments have 144 golfers, which necessitates starting two foursomes on each hole.

Big tournaments like this often designate those foursomes as "A" and "B." This just means that the "A" group plays the hole first, followed by the "B" group.

If you're playing in a tournament that uses handicaps — golf 's way of evening out the differences between players of different skill levels — your total **gross score** is adjusted to a **net score**. In other words, if your gross score is, say, 105, it will be lower after your handicap is factored in and the score adjusted. You could even end up with a score under par!

Mulligans

Aye, a term known by every golfer. In any language, a mulligan is a do-over. A second chance. A freebie. In casual golf, a couple mulligans per round tends to be the accepted norm. However, some unwritten rules apply. As a beginner, take a mulligan or provisional shot when your ball is possibly out of bounds and most likely won't be found. Do not take a mulligan just to try and improve a less than perfect shot. Just play your ball… and go to the driving range for practice. Mulligans are often sold at tournaments to raise additional money for a charity.

NOTE: *If you don't have an official handicap, no problem! Just inform the tournament organizers or a tournament official that you are a beginning golfer and have not established a handicap yet. They will give you one, and it will be the max!*

Stroke play, also called medal play, is the most basic golf format. It is exactly what the name implies — each player counts all her strokes on each hole and tallies them at the end of the round.

Match play is a format as old as the game itself, and puts the focus on individual holes rather than your overall total score. Each hole is a separate competition. This means, if you have a blow-up hole, it isn't a big deal — it's only one hole.

In match play you win the hole, lose the hole, or tie the hole. The scoring is expressed as **all square** (meaning the players are tied),

1-up, 2-up, etc. The match is over when one player is "up" by more holes than there are left to play. A final score of "3 and 2," for example, means one player was up by 3 holes and there were only two holes left to play.

I'm Scrambling!

My friend Chris phoned in a panic! Her biggest client had invited her to play in his foursome in a golf tournament. She had explained to him that she never played except for one time about ten years ago, but he wouldn't take "No" for an answer.

I told her the good news was that he knew she didn't play. There would be no expectations of her. Chris was fun to be around, and her client wanted her on the team because of her personality.

The next week brought another panicked call from Chris. The client had just invited Greg, Chris' coworker, to play in the foursome. "Greg is an amazing golfer, Debbie! His office is full of golf paraphernalia! He talks about golf all the time! I can't do this. I don't want to embarrass myself in front of him!"

We talked it through and she decided she'd play. I asked her to call me afterward to let me know how it went.

She called a few days after the tournament, laughing. She'd had a great time! It was a scramble tournament and she putted first for her team on each hole, to give them the line. One putt was very long and she made it. Her teammates were high-fiving and bragged about her at the dinner that evening. And Greg, she said, was "…terrible! He hit his ball far, but I don't think he EVER hit the fairway! We spent a lot of time looking for his balls in the desert."

Chris ended the call with, "I'm never going to miss one of these again!"

And neither should you!

Bet You'll Enjoy These Games Too!

"What are we playing today?" is a question often heard on the first tee just prior to a group of golfers beginning their round. Even the newest golfer will sense that the question adds a little extra excitement to the air, because we all have a competitive spirit. Most golfers enjoy the additional challenge of a friendly wager, but don't panic. Every golfer knows you win sometimes, and sometimes you lose, but it's always fun either way.

There are many different betting games and they fall into one of two categories: games that use player handicaps when calculating the scores, and games that do not. Beginning or less skilled players often have not played enough rounds of golf to establish an official handicap, so games that use handicaps or "guestimated" handicaps may at first sound more intimidating than fun.

When you're hosting a round of golf, betting games can help you control the energy in your foursome. Depending on the game you choose to play, you can ease the pressure and enhance everyone's experience for a memorable day. Remember to take into consideration the skill levels of your group and choose a game best suited to forwarding relationships and ensuring a good time is had by all.

Here are a few popular betting games that do not use handicaps:

- *Bingo, Bango, Bongo* is a game in which players try to accumulate points, with three possible points to be won on each hole — one point for being first to get a ball on the green (Bingo), one point for having the approach shot closest to the pin (Bango) and one point for making the longest putt (Bongo). At the end of the round each player totals her points, which each are worth an amount of money agreed upon before play begins. Say each point is worth 10¢. If you won every point on every hole, you'd win a total of $5.40 from your playing partners.

An easy way to remember the objective of this game is First On, Closest to the Pin, Longest Putt. Assign someone to keep track of the points and clarify the results of each hole prior to playing the next hole.

- *Greenies* is a game played on par 3 holes. The objective is to be closest to the pin, but in order to win the bet — typically $1 from each player — the player closest to the pin must make par or better.

  If no one lands a ball on the green or if the player closest to the hole doesn't make par or better, the money can carry over to the next par 3 hole or the bet simply ends with no winner (players should decide before the first par 3 hole is played whether the bets will carry over).

- *Poleys* is a putting game in which a player wins a point for making a putt that is longer than the length of the flagstick. A player can win two points by chipping in from off the green — a "double poley!"

  Points won by each player are totaled at the end of the round and the winner receives a pre-determined amount from each player, typically $1 or $2.

Betting games that do <u>require players to have a handicap</u> or "guestimated" handicap:

- *Skins* is a game in which the best net score on each hole wins money.

  Prior to teeing off on the first hole establish each player's course handicap and the value of each skin. If each skin is worth $1, the most you could lose is $18.

  The player making the best net score wins the skin on each hole. If there is a tie, the money carries over to the next hole.

- *Nassau* is a very common game that consists of three competitions in one — the front nine score, the back nine score, and the overall total score.

  Start by determining the amount of the bet. Typical bets for Nassau are $2:

  - $2 for the front nine
  - $2 for the back
  - $2 for the overall total

A team or player who is losing has the right to "press the bet," in essence starting another bet to (hopefully) offset the one that she is currently losing. This is a second bet, then, that begins when the player declares she is pressing. Multiple presses complicate things and ratchet up the excitement!

- *Stableford* is a way of scoring that is commonly used in Europe. Its advantage is that you can have a bad hole and not be out of the match because of it.

You are awarded points based on your score for each hole (determine in advance whether you are using gross scores or net scores). Typically, points are awarded as follows:

- 1 for a net bogey
- 2 for a net par
- 3 for a net birdie
- 5 for a net eagle
- 8 for a net albatross

Total each player's points at the end of the round. The winner—the player with the most points—claims the purse, an amount of money determined prior to the round, $5 from each player, for example.

All these games are among the most popular, and you can find many other favorites such as Wolf (handicaps used) and Animals (no handicaps), along with their rules, on the internet.

Things to do after your round of golf:

- Remember to pay all your bets. How you handle your financial affairs on the golf course is an indication of how you do business. You don't want to be caught "forgetting" to pay up or collect.

- The winner usually buys the drinks at the 19th hole — spending all the money she won and then some!

- Don't be surprised if, when you're a guest or the fourth in a new group, payment doesn't happen, but rather they're all looking for bragging rights.

- If you're a woman playing with men, don't be surprised if they are chivalrous and refuse your money. That's fine. Yet, do your best to always insist on paying!

A word for the wise...

"Never bet with anyone you meet on the first tee who has a deep suntan, a one-iron in his bag, and squinty eyes."

~ *Dave Marr, 1965 PGA Champion*

The Blueprint For Success

"I recently participated in a scramble for the American Institute of Architects local chapter. My boss knows I am learning the game. He and I were paired with two 20-something architects who announced on the first tee that they intended to win the tournament as they had in the past. This bummed me out a little since I had to inform them I was a beginner. They said it was no big deal since our scores would be handicapped. We won the tournament! 13-under net score! They used two of my drives, one chip to the green and one putt. What a fun day! The best part was, they commented on how great it was to play with a beginner who appreciated pace of play and knew the rules and etiquette."

Allison Suriano
Architect

They Call Me "The Drainorator"

"I couldn't wait to get into the office today so I could talk about the golf tournament I was in on Saturday. I wasn't terrific or anything, but it sure felt good knowing I had absorbed so much information from [the golf clinic]. The biggest surprise came on the green. My teammates called me the "drainorator" because I kept sinking so many long putts!"

Jessica Boutwell
Co-Owner
Růže Cake House

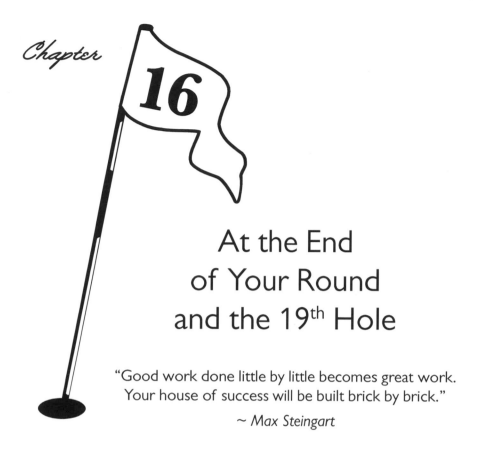

Chapter

16

At the End of Your Round and the 19ᵗʰ Hole

"Good work done little by little becomes great work.
Your house of success will be built brick by brick."

~ Max Steingart

On your last hole, when everyone has holed their balls, shake your playing partners' hands and thank them for the round. It is customary for gentlemen to remove their caps while doing so. Just like finishing your golf swing, this is the time to set up your follow through. Let a person know you are going to call about something specific, or ask him or her if they have time to meet in the clubhouse (also known as the 19ᵗʰ Hole) for a drink or a bite to eat.

When you return your carts to the staging area, many courses have attendants ready to **clean your clubs** with a wet towel. If tipping is allowed, $2 - $5 per bag is appropriate. If you are the host, cover the tip for your guest(s). Note that this tip is not just for cleaning your clubs — it is for removing your clubs from the car and putting them on a cart, putting them back into your car when you leave, and

preparing your cart for the round with a scorecard, pencil, cups, towel, etc. Even if you don't have your clubs cleaned, it is still customary to tip the outside staff for all they have done (they pool their tips, like waiters).

Before you leave your cart, definitely double-check to make sure you have all your personal belongings. You'd be amazed how many cell phones, keys and sunglasses get left behind.

If the cart had any issues — bad brakes, lack of power — inform the attendant so they can get those things fixed before the next golfer takes the cart out.

Do a quick inventory of your bag. Count your clubs to make sure they are all there. Are you missing any head covers? Will you need to resupply your bag with tees or balls before your next round? Make a mental note, if necessary.

If you and your guests gather in the 19th hole after your round, take the lead and cover the first round — unless you've been buying beverages on the course. In that case, your playing partners are likely to pick up the tab in the clubhouse.

The clubhouse is the proper place to firm up any business connections that you made during the round. Exchange business cards, swap contact information — whatever you can do to forward the relationship. If appropriate, schedule a phone call or, if possible, a time and place to meet for lunch.

Playing Golf Can Be Good for Business

It is no secret that people like doing business with people they know, and one of the best places for getting to know someone is a golf course. But, if you think large business deals or sales are made on a golf course, think again. More commonly, a golf outing is a catalyst for developing and enhancing relationships that lead to business transactions.

Here are ten tips to help you make the most of your next corporate outing:

1. *Think about the player(s) you're inviting and your objectives.* Remember that one of the best things you can do for a client or prospect is introduce him or her to a prospect.

2. *Pick the right event/setting.* The venue you choose should match the skill level of your playing partners (and yours). A WOW! golf course may be too challenging and not fun. If the outing is a golf tournament, verify the playing format and be sure it fits your guests' skillsets. A scramble might be preferable to a best-ball or shamble format, for example.

3. *Introduce the players to one another* prior to the outing and give each one information about the course and/or event. Consider sharing websites and LinkedIn contacts.

4. *Bring a gift for your playing partners.* A sleeve of balls with your logo is always appropriate. Check with your marketing department for branded items left over from other events. The gift can be anything that is thoughtful. You could also buy the first round of drinks, even if it is bottled water.

5. *Help others have their best round possible.* This has to do with adhering to proper golf etiquette — not talking when another player is hitting; standing to the side rather than directly behind a player who is hitting; turning your cell phone off; not walking through another player's putting line on the green. In other words, don't be the scapegoat for someone's bad shot.

6. *If your group is playing different sets of tees, join your partners on their teeing ground(s).* This creates opportunities for conversation to and from the tee, builds camaraderie and puts extra eyes on the direction of tee shots, which helps pace of play.

7. *Bring business cards.* Always keep a stack in your golf bag. And an extra pen or pencil. You can make notations on a player's business card — a reminder of something you spoke about, or an idea to bring up after the round.

8. ***Show your best self.*** You are observing others, but they are observing you too. Mind your mannerisms, discussion topics, even your risky shots (you can be seen as a risk-taker, but never a fool). Dress appropriately. And especially be careful with the amount of alcohol you consume. Alcohol and warm temperatures are a bad combination. Remember that the more you drink, the looser and louder the conversation.

9. ***Maintain a good Pace of Play.*** Nobody likes a straggler.

10. ***Manage your time.*** This is important in a couple of ways: first, be on time — people who show up late with their hair on fire and a mouthful of excuses are neither amusing nor endearing; second, don't leave immediately after the round. The post-round time is your opportunity to explore synergies for business, follow up on a specific issue discussed during the round, or plant a seed or schedule an appointment. Think of this time as your chance to take a big swing and follow through!

Go ahead... Turn Golf into Gold®

My Playing Partners Weren't Criminals, But Might Know Some

"No matter what business you are in, getting new work is all about new relationships. In a previous career I was a criminal defense lawyer. My playing partners were not likely to need my services the next day, but they could pass my name along. And they did. The game of golf is an ideal networking tool because it reaches into so many areas of interest and offers something for everyone."

Debbie Hill
Attorney and Consultant
President, La Cerra Sueno LLC

Playing with Men

"Trousers may be worn by women golfers
on the course, but must be taken off
on entering the clubhouse."

~ *English Golf Club Sign, 1907*

The golf industry was built by catering to the needs of male golfers. That's not an indictment, just a relevant point when considering how women's participation in golf is growing. Women continue to be the largest group coming into the game. Golf course designers are beginning to address the fact that men and women are different. *Vive la différence!*

Golf increases your opportunities in the business world. There's no doubt about it. Yet, women DO NOT need golf for networking with other women. Women network successfully with each other over a cup of coffee, a wine tasting, a trunk show, a charity event — the list goes on. Women support and do business with other women.

What golf can give you in more male-oriented business settings is a place on the radar screen. You're included in the conversation. And you have more power in your dealings with men, since golf enables you to cross over easily into one of their favorite "business" environments. This is why women need to learn not only how to play golf, but how to play with men. (And men need to learn how to play with women.)

Playing golf with men will amuse you, delight you, and invigorate you! Know going in that many men believe they should play from the **back tees** because, well, you know, they hit the ball so far. What you'll see, more often than not, is that they do hit it far. Far to the left, far to the right — far in every direction but down the middle of the fairway.

You should also know that often, men spend quite a bit of time searching for their golf balls. (There are exceptions to that generalization, of course.) Be patient with them. Maintain your pace of play and demonstrate at least a rudimentary understanding of golf 's etiquette and rules — and men will think you are a FABULOUS golf partner.

Trust me on this. I've experienced it and heard it from hundreds, if not thousands, of women.

As I mentioned, most men will not play from the Forward Tees. So, if you're playing from the forward set of tees and the men are not, join them on their teeing area as they hit. You'll not only be able to bird dog where their balls land, helping the pace of play, but you'll create even more opportunities to build camaraderie.

If the teeing area is not right next to the cart path, then, when it's your turn, ask someone to join you on the tee to help you watch your ball — even if you have great eyes. This can lead to still more relationship building.

Be prepared for your male playing partners to occasionally forget that you have not hit and drive right past your forward tees. It happens. They will be embarrassed and make a joke about it. Laugh with them, at them, for them. Keep a smile on your face.

Men love to help women on the golf course. They'll hunt for your balls, even clean them for you. And they delight in offering advice.

Unsolicited swing advice, though, is the worst! If you *want* the input, great. Tell them you are open to suggestions.

If you're not looking for pointers, however, it can quickly become uncomfortable to have someone critiquing your form. Thinking about your swing as you hit is ideal at the driving range – but it can paralyze you when you're on the course. In this case, a great way to curb on-course advice is to tell your playing partners that you're taking lessons (whether or not that's true!) and that your pro has you working on something new. Not only will your impromptu teacher(s) back off, they'll be impressed that you're taking lessons.

Some women tell me they are reluctant to invite a man to play golf for fear it may give the wrong impression. I ask them whether it would be wrong to invite a man to lunch, and they say it would not. Remember that, especially in professional contexts, a round of golf is no different than meeting for lunch. To address their concerns about a man coming on to them, I suggest what I do when I play with men — I bring up my husband (who rocks my world!), my kids, etc. That always makes it clear.

Just a thought: in general, men approach golf with a vision of conquering the game. They focus on the score, distances, winning, betting games, statistics. Most women approach golf in order to create relationships around the game. Be aware of what motivates your playing partners. Be graceful, respectful and attentive. Help them have their best day possible on the golf course, and you'll have friends for life!

Oh — one more thing about playing with men. Ladies, you know how we are. We love to *talk*. Men, not so much. On the golf course, be mindful of this. You know the old saying — if someone asks you what time it is, don't explain how to build a watch.

Tee Time for Two

"My husband, Chris, and I always take our clubs along when we travel. Golf gives us a connection with the local landscape that we wouldn't get if we just remained in tourist hot spots. Most importantly, it is a connection with locals who share unique stories about life where they live while we are enjoying a round of golf with them. Golf is a great connector. I have worked with golf development companies for almost 30 years and have seen how lasting friendships and productive business associations develop from a few rounds of golf. The game also is a great equalizer. With a little experience, everyone who stands over the ball has an opportunity to hit a solid drive down the fairway or an errant shot into the weeds. You learn quickly that there are valuable lessons for life in the game of golf. Here's one: forget about your most recent mistake and move on to your next shot, or let it overwhelm you and ruin your day."

Mary Alexander
Executive VP and General Counsel
DMB Development LLC

I Made It a Policy to Play Golf with Men

"It was job-related. A majority of the people in my capacity in the insurance industry are men, and insurance meetings always include a golf outing. I wanted to be part of it. The wives go shopping or sightseeing; the men play golf. The first few meetings I traveled to, I discovered that while I was out shopping, the men were playing golf — and talking business. When we all gathered again in the evening I'd ask the men if we were going to discuss xyz tomorrow, and they'd say, 'We already talked about that today on the golf course.'"

Jean Ann Morris
Senior Vice President
Wells Fargo Insurance Services

Get Your Golf On
and Go Places

"There is nothing like stepping onto a golf course
on a clear, fresh morning."

~ *Kathy Whitworth*

Golf is a fantastic vehicle for establishing and developing meaningful personal and professional relationships. It opens doors almost effort-lessly. Mention that you play golf to almost any new friend, colleague, client or prospect and you don't just get your foot in the door — you're pulled into the house, so to speak.

The game also provides a wonderful environment for exploring and honing your own skills, strategies and character. You find that it enriches your life in myriad ways. Ask any golfer why she plays and you'll hear her love of the game in her answer. There is just something magical that happens when you hit that little white ball and see it go high and far and right where you envisioned (even if it happens only one time during the outing!).

What Can You Do with Golf?

- **Experience quality time.** You'll experience several hours of undivided attention from clients, business associates, prospects, employees, friends, spouses, relatives, and even strangers.

- **Develop relationships.** Rather than just meeting across a table for lunch, golf enables you to participate, commiserate and celebrate together. You'll be amazed at how well you can further a relationship without the confinement of business attire and a desk.

- **Learn about others.** Golf does a remarkable job of revealing a person's temperament. How does she react under pressure? What does she like to talk about? Is she respectful? Does she make excuses? Would you consider sending her business or referrals?

- **Challenge yourself.** Most executives are bright and strategy-minded, and golf may be the ultimate game in that respect: it's a constant test of how well you handle the unique circumstances presented by each hole or each shot.

- **Learn a new skill.** Learning never gets old; in fact, learning keeps you interested in yourself and interesting to others. Learning to play golf grows your personal skill set and broadens your professional reach.

- **Network more easily.** Golf is as close as you get to a magical buzzword. If you hear someone talking about their game, someone else's game or just the game in general, it's an instant opportunity to form a bond — and maybe even get a foot in the door.

- **Connect with nature.** Golf course scenery and surroundings are serene and inviting. Even a well-worn municipal course puts a blue sky over your head and offers a break from the day-to-day grind.

- **Think charitably.** Golf offers myriad opportunities to make an impact and give something back to the community. Whether you play, sponsor or volunteer on a committee, participating in a charity tournament can bring you and your company invaluable community recognition.

- **Reconnect with your family.** Golf is a game that can be enjoyed by young and old alike. It's also something you do together — the perfect excuse for a regular reunion with kids, parents or grandparents!

This last thing you can do with golf, reconnecting with your family, is especially meaningful to me. If you've ever watched an elderly couple dancing at, say, a 60th wedding anniversary, you know how they are carried away by the music, seemingly freed from their aches and pains. For an evening, a few hours or even just a few moments, they experience a transformation. I saw this same thing when I played golf with Maury.

Maury was in his 90s. He didn't always trust his balance and shuffled a bit more than he walked. He would grab a handrail if one was handy, or a shoulder, if necessary. But it wasn't just out of concern that I kept an eye on Maury at the golf course. He taught me things.

Maury played from the forward tees. I watched when he bent over to put a tee in the ground. He was slow and methodical about this, resourceful and efficient too — while he was down there, he always checked for other tees lying on the ground and picked up the keepers. It made me smile when he did this. It was Maury being a kid. *Transformation.*

I thought about a lot of things when I played with Maury. I thought about how free of ego and everyday concerns he seemed to be. If only all golfers would play the tees appropriate to their skill levels instead of the tees that satisfy their egos. It would help them enjoy the game more, and it would help every foursome behind them. A foursome playing the wrong tees slows everyone else down.

When Maury hit a ball into the rough, he would mutter something to himself because he always hoped for a fairway landing, but I know he was not entirely disappointed. I would even say he was not disappointed at all, because Maury loved finding golf balls. He found his ball, my ball, any ball — even balls the group playing the next fairway over were looking for.

On our 9th and final hole, Maury would carefully line up his putt, but sinking it didn't really matter. He was on the golf course. That is what mattered. Maury, my mother and I always left the last green arm-in-arm. When we did, I invariably thought ahead to the next time when I would bring them to the dance floor and set them free to roll back the years.

There are many reasons to play golf, and the reasons change with the years. If I were asked my number one reason right now, I'm not sure what I'd say, but on the days I played with Maury, I knew it with certainty: You live longer.

The Gift of Golf

During a long-ago brief vacation at the beach, the famous author Anne Morrow Lindbergh was inspired by shells she picked up to write Gift from the Sea, a beautiful collection of contemplations and musings about the mysteries of a woman's life. I often see that this wonderful game of golf I love is a similar kind of gift. It just keeps giving in so many ways!

Take what golf does for "sorority sisters" Lois and Sally. They meet every Sunday morning at the golf course and clearly enjoy each other's company. Neither of the two envisions playing a spectacular round, but that's not why they come. Like every golfer, they'd like to play well, but their objective is just to spend time together away from the hard task of caretaking. Lois' husband is in assisted living;

Sally's should be. Golf is a gift they give each other, every Sunday, rain or shine.

What has golf gifted to you? *Here's how others have answered:*

- Tony enjoys that it's socially acceptable to drink beer.
- Jill loves golf because it's how she met her husband.
- Taba, like Jill, met her life partner through golf and now summers in Ireland.
- Silver, who has many friends who play golf, is inspired by Jill and Taba and looks forward to meeting her life partner on the golf course.
- Joyce loves the friends she's met through golf.
- Mary loves golf because she's so darn competitive and can beat the boys.
- Dan declares his love for golf, the second-best stress reliever he knows.
- Susan enjoys league play — she has something to look forward to every Thursday.
- Gerry loves golf but wishes that golf loved him.
- Danny loves the views… she lives on a golf course.
- Caroline loves golf because she can spend time with her mom.
- Dwight loves golf because he can't play it inside his office.
- Ann likes the shoes… and the shopping.
- Tim loves that every time he goes out to play, he can beat the crap out of something 105 times!
- Le Ann loves golf because not only is it her avocation, it's her vocation. She feels very lucky to work in the golf industry!
- Larry loves golf because it's turned him into a travel writer and the perks are fabulous!
- Ron loves golf because he gets to be with his friends and meet some new and "interesting" people.

- Chris enjoys having an activity to do with his lovely wife in addition to hiking.

- Gary loves that golf is unique — both men and women can play, even when our bodies are falling apart; it's a sport that we can still feel young again.

- Larry loves that playing golf is like taking a vacation with three other friends, male and female, without interruptions.

- Helen (Larry's wife) loves golf because she can have a sweet time with her husband and still continue to talk.

You can't wrap it, but golf is surely a beautiful gift!

It's Okay! Tips For Having Fun Playing Golf

1. *It's okay to not keep score.*

2. *It's okay to play from the most forward set of tees or start at the 150-yard marker.*

3. *It's okay to give yourself a better lie by rolling the ball around a little.*

4. *It's okay to tee the ball up anywhere when you are first learning.*

5. *It's okay to count swings only when you make contact with the ball.*

6. *It's okay to throw the ball out of a bunker after one try.*

7. *It's okay to forget about a ball that may be lost or out of bounds. It's okay to drop a ball where you think it might be... or where you wanted it to be.*

8. *It's okay to play a scramble with your group — scrambles are very popular.*

9. *It's okay to just chip and putt on a hole when you feel like it.*

10. *It's okay to pick up in the middle of the hole and enjoy the outdoors and scenery.*

11. *It's okay to skip a hole if you need to take a break.*

12. *It's okay to play less than 9 or 18 holes and call it a round of golf.*

13. It's okay to move your ball away from trees, rocks or very hilly lies.

14. It's okay to hit the same club for the entire round, while using a putter on the putting green.

15. It's okay to play golf in your sneakers. Be comfortable!

16. It's okay to get enthusiastic! (High fives, fist pumps and big smiles are encouraged)

17. It's okay to talk on the golf course — enjoy a nice conversation or tell a few jokes.

18. It's okay to bring your kids to the course whether they are 5 or 35.

19. It's okay to PLAY GOLF JUST FOR FUN! Play the set of tees that make you the happiest.

20. It's okay to laugh and have fun. There are no penalties for excessive laughing or high fives on the golf course.

21. It's okay to gamble some — and laugh even more.

22. It's okay to remember friends more than your scores.

23. It's okay that your love of the game lasts longer than that for a past "significant other."

24. It's okay to play your favorite music on every hole.

25. It's okay to play barefoot golf — shoes optional.

26. It's okay to coordinate your attire — but still wear your hat backwards.

27. It's okay to drink more than one cup of water on a hot day.

28. It's okay to have your spouse or significant other outdrive you every hole when he or she plays from forward tees.

29. It's okay to wear your favorite sports team's uniform (college or pro) when you play golf.

30. It's okay to turn OFF your cell phone while on the course.

31. It's okay to "Drive for Show" — and still not putt for dough.

32. It's okay to create your own charity golf event to raise dollars for good causes.

33. It's okay to be called a "golfer."

So, What Are You Waiting For?

Well, all that's left to do now is **Get Your Golf On!** There are a lot of ways to get in the game and clue others in on the fact that you "know your golf." Here are some tips to help you get started:

1) Start talking!

a. Bring up golf in conversations. Keep the excitement alive. Find information to talk about.

   i. Discuss your own experiences; ask others about their experiences

   ii. Listen/watch *Golf Channel* and the *PGA Channel* on *Sirius/XM Radio* — be a sponge! Pick up things via osmosis

   iii. Read the golf section in your local newspaper — might appear just one day a week in the sports pages

   iv. Read golf magazines

   v. Join LinkedIn groups and read on-line blogs

   vi. Listen to radio shows like *RadioGolfClub.com* or *Blog-TalkRadio.com/WomenOfGolf*

   vii. Read on-line newsletters like *womensgolf.com*, *gottagogolf.com* and *lpga.com/lpga-newsletters*

2) Surround yourself with golf things.

a. If you work in an office, add a golf book or trophy to your credenza, put a putter in the corner, place a photo of you and your friends at the golf course on your desk

b. Subscribe to a golf magazine

c. Wear your golf clothes on and off the course

3) And by all means, participate and play!

a. Find a golf group in your area that offers clinics, leagues and programs for new golfers, especially women — it's so easy to participate in already existing programs. And if it feels safer, grab a friend to join you!

    i. Local Golf Association in your state or community

    ii. LPGA Women's Network, LPGA Amateur Golf Association, *LPGA.com, #inviteHER*

    iii. "Find a Teacher" link on the LPGA website, *LPGA.com/tcp*

    iv. Play Golf America, *playgolfamerica.com*

    v. Get Golf Ready, *GetGolfReady.com*

    vi. Call a few nearby golf courses and ask about their clinics and programming for beginning or female golfers

    vii. The Latina Golfers Association, *LatinaGolfers.com*

    viii. Women of Color Golf, *womenofcolorgolf.org*

    ix. Participate in Women's Golf Day, the first Tuesday in June, *WomensGolfDay.com*

    x. Ask friends for recommendations

b. Take individual golf lessons

c. Visit the driving range

d. Volunteer on a charity golf tournament committee

e. Play in a charity golf tournament

f. Attend a professional golf tournament – PGA, LPGA, Champions Tour, Legends Tour, Korn Ferry Tour, Symetra Tour, Canadian Tour, mini tour events in your area

g. Attend a conference or serminar that incorporates golf and life tips, like *teamaureus.com*

h. Involve the children in your life

    i.   The First Tee

    ii. PGA Junior League

    iii. Drive, Chip and Putt

    iv. LPGA*USGA Girls Golf

    v. Junior clinics offered at golf courses in your area

That Was Fast!

"I had played golf a few times casually with friends in my first year of business school, but it was just something to do, not a regular activity for me. It never occurred to me to take lessons until I learned a Women's Leadership group on campus was offering free golf lessons. A few classmates and I decided to give it a try. The instructor was Char Carson, an LPGA Teaching Professional. One of the things she told us is that golf can be a great marketing tool for professional women. Soon after that I was interviewing with a company for a consultant position in supply chain management. Almost as an aside I was asked whether I play golf. I said, "Yes!" I added that I was taking golf lessons. It wasn't even a formal question, but it felt like a nice additional touch point. Our conversation then steered into a golf discussion, and it was an Aha! moment for me. The interviewer acknowledged that it was a male-driven industry, but because I could play golf I already had a huge leg up in the business. Char was right!

Zoe M. Gryparis
Arizona State University/W. P. Carey School of Business
MBA candidate, class of 2019

Golf Buddies

"At the team's first practice each year I ask the girls why they have come out for golf. One response I always hear is, "She," pointing, "asked me to do it with her!" Golf is a wonderful game played by individuals, but buddies are what make it fun—practice after practice, match after match, round after round throughout life. It's such a unique sport, and for new golfers it can be intimidating, but the pressure's off and intimidation disappears when you have a buddy doing it with you. I don't have to teach anyone how to have fun playing golf; the game creates it. Our girls and boys practice together and occasionally we match them together. They like the challenge! Some girls come out because they want to understand the game better or because they know it's something they can do with mom or dad. One 15-year-old was thinking way ahead when she said, 'I just want to get better so when I get older I can play with my old lady friends.'"

Jason Glashan
Girls Golf Coach
Notre Dame Preparatory High School

One Last Word of Advice...

I have met and continue to meet the most fascinating and wonderful people through my engagement with the game of golf. I've developed friendships with people I otherwise never would have met and gained insights that I otherwise never would have realized. One special joy in my life is playing golf with my husband, Jack — not only because it gives us time together, but for the adventures we share seeking out and playing courses wherever we travel.

When technology and busyness — computers, commutes, cell phones and deadlines — become too much a part of my daily life, golf takes me away to beautiful surroundings, a change of focus, and uninterrupted time to breathe and daydream and enjoy a round with golf buddies.

I am humbled by my journey with the game and the opportunity it gives me to be in the right place, at the right time, to encourage others, especially women, as they get their first taste of golf or give golf another chance. It is so delightful to watch them grow not only as golfers but as women, developing real confidence that will carry over into other parts of their lives.

And to think I once believed so strongly that golf was boring!

Golf Lingo Glossary

Ace: A hole-in-one. Hitting the ball into the hole in one stroke.

Address: Taking a stance and placing the clubhead behind the golf ball in preparation for playing a shot.

Aerating/aerification: A preventative maintenance process by which very small holes are punched into the grass on the golf course to provide growing room for grass roots and to help keep turfgrass healthy.

Albatross: A score of three less than par — as you can imagine, a very rare occurrence! You'll also hear "double eagle." It's the same thing as an albatross.

Alternate shot: A golf competition format in which two golfers play as partners playing one golf ball, taking turns playing the strokes.

Animals: A betting game played over nine holes or reset at the turn for the second nine using names of animals to track situations that happen on the golf course within your group.

Apron: The shorter grass directly in front of the green.

All square: When the score is tied in match play.

Away: The ball that's farthest away from the hole, as in "you're away." The player farthest away typically hits first.

Back nine: The second nine holes of golf on an 18-hole golf course, typically holes 10-18.

Back swing: The initial part of the golf swing in which the player moves the club away from its initial position behind the golf ball.

Back tees: The farthest set of tees from the hole on each hole, also referred to as "the tips."

Ball marker: A coin-sized object, typically round, used to mark the position of a player's ball on the green.

Ball mark: A small indentation on the surface of a green resulting from the impact of a golf ball.

Beach: Slang term for a sand bunker.

Bentgrass: A type of grass used on golf courses, especially known for allowing balls to run smoothly and quickly on the greens.

Bermuda grass: A popular variety of grass used on golf courses.

Best ball: A format of play typically used in tournaments, in which the team score for each hole is the "best score" of at least one of the players in a foursome. "Best ball" is often mistaken for Scramble.

Bingo, Bango, Bongo: A fun betting game in which 3 points are available on each hole — one for the first person to land a ball on the green (Bingo), one for the ball that is closest to the hole once all players' balls are on the green (Bango) and one for the longest putt made (Bongo).

Birdie: A score of one less than par.

Bite: A ball with lots of backspin is said to "bite," since it stays pretty close to where it landed or even spins back toward the player. Sometimes a player will shout (pray) for a ball to bite if it looks like it's going past the hole. (A humorous way of doing this is to shout, "Grow teeth!")

Bogey: A score of one over par.

Bracket: To take additional clubs — one higher and one lower — than the club you believe you need to hit a certain shot. This means you'll be prepared for a situation different from what you originally expected, so it's generally a good idea.

Break: The curve or bend in a putt due to the slope of the terrain.

Bump and run: A low-trajectory golf shot intended to send the ball rolling along the ground and onto the green.

Bunker: A concave area containing sand or the like.

Caddie: A person who carries a golfer's bag and clubs and provides insightful advice and moral support to the golfer.

Cart path: A path lining and connecting the holes on a golf course on which golf carts drive.

Cart path only: A condition on the golf course by which players driving motorized golf carts must drive only on the cart paths and not on the grass.

Casual water: An accumulation of water on the golf course that is not part of a penalty area. Generally, you encounter casual water after heavy rains. The player is allowed to move the ball without penalty.

Chipping: A low-trajectory, short golf shot typically made from just off the green.

Choke down: When a player places his/her grip lower down the shaft of the golf club than normal.

Club fitting: The process of measuring a golfer's physical dimensions and swing speed, then building clubs to match. Club fitting assures a golfer's equipment will have the proper length, lie and shaft flex, eliminating many hitting errors attributed to clubs not custom fit to player.

Course handicap: A number that indicates how many strokes a player receives on a specific golf course and from a specific set of tees.

Cup: The four-inch deep, 4.5-inch diameter hole on the green.

Cut shot: A golf shot in which the ball gradually moves left to right (for a right-handed golfer). Also known as a "fade."

Dance floor: Slang term for the green.

Deep: A flagstick or hole that is located toward the back of the green.

Distance measuring device: A tool that allows a player to measure distances on the golf course — commonly a GPS watch, a handheld rangefinder, a Smartphone App, etc.

Divot: The small chunk of turf that is dislodged when a clubhead strikes the ground as a player hits the ball.

Divot repair tool: A small metal or plastic tool with a prong(s), used to repair ball marks on the green.

Divot seed mixture: A mixture of typically sand, seed and soil that a player can place into a divot on the teeing area or fairway.

Dog leg: A golf hole that is crooked and not straight. Dogleg right refers to a hole that bends to the right.

Double bogey: A score of two over par. Generally shortened to "a double."

Down swing: The downward movement of the golf club – the portion of the swing prior to making contact with the golf ball.

Drained: Slang term for having sunk a putt.

Draw: A golf shot in which the ball gradually moves right to left (for a right-handed golfer).

Drive: The first shot taken at the teeing area at each hole — even if you don't hit it with a Driver.

Driver: The longest club (and the one with the biggest head), used for tee shots as it's designed to hit the ball the farthest.

Drop area: A special designated area in which a player may choose to drop his/her ball as an option after hitting his/her ball into a penalty area.

Duff: A bad shot.

Duck hook: When a right-handed player strikes the ball such that it curves sharply from right to left and stays low to the ground.

Eagle: A score of two under par.

Etiquette: The rules governing a golfer's behavior.

Executive course: A golf course that is shorter and has a lower par than regular golf courses. Consisting of mostly par-3 holes, it is designed to be played quickly by skilled golfers and to be welcoming for beginner golfers and juniors.

Fade: A golf shot in which the ball gradually moves left to right (for a right-handed golfer). Sometimes called "a cut shot."

Fairway: The center, short-mown portion of a golf hole in between the teeing area and the green.

Fat: A shot in which the club hits the ground (more so than intended) prior to striking the ball. Sometimes also called "thick" or "chunked."

First tee: Where a round of golf play begins.

Flag/Flag stick: The flag is a piece of fabric attached to the top of the flagstick so that golfers can see where the hole is located. The flagstick is a pole placed in the center of the hole on the green.

Flyer: A ball, usually hit from the rough, that goes much farther than intended.

Fly the green: A shot that goes over the green.

Follow through: The part of the golf swing (or putting stroke) after the ball is struck.

Foot wedge: kicking the ball (which, of course, is against the Rules) in order to improve the position of the golf ball.

Fore: A warning shouted when the ball is heading toward a person.

Foursome: A group of four players.

Forward tee: The teeing area located closest to the green.

Fried egg: Typically in a sand bunker, when the ball is half-buried such that it resembles a fried egg.

Fringe: The short grass surrounding the green that is kept slightly longer than the grass on the green.

Front nine: The first nine holes of an 18-hole golf course.

Get up: A phrase shouted at a ball that looks like it's going to land short of the target. If it looks like it's going to land in a difficult spot (perhaps water or a bunker), you'd say "get over."

Gimme: A putt that is so close to the hole that it's assumed that the player will make it. You can only have a "gimme" in casual, non-tournament play or in match play and it does count as a stroke. An old-fashioned term for this is "in the leather," a reference to the ball being closer to the hole than the length of a putter from the putter's face to the bottom of its grip.

Grain: The direction that grass on the green is growing. The golf ball rolls faster with the grain and slower against the grain.

Green fee: The cost to play a round of golf. (This usually includes the cost of the golf cart rental and practice balls.) Some golfers use the term "greens fee" (plural), but the proper term is "green fee."

Green in regulation (GIR): When the golf ball lands on the green in two less shots than the par assigned to that hole. For instance, landing on the green in one shot on a par 3 hole or two shots on a par 4 hole.

Greenies: A betting game in which money goes to the player whose ball is on the green and closest to the hole on a Par 3, so long as the player scores a par or better.

Grip: There are two meanings to the word grip as it relates to golf. One refers to how someone places his or her hands onto the golf club; a technique of holding onto the club. The other refers to the covering around the end of the golf club that helps the golfer hold onto the club without it slipping through the hands when swinging.

Gross Score: The total number of strokes you take during your round of golf, plus any penalty strokes. Deducting your handicap from your gross score gives your net score. Golf competitions and friendly betting games are often based on your net score.

Ground under repair: Any part of the golf course marked by stakes or a painted line, which might be damaged or undergoing maintenance such that it is unfit for play.

Grounding: Setting the heel of the golf club on the ground, however briefly.

Halfway house: A structure located typically between the 9th and 10th holes, which provides snacks and refreshments for golfers.

Handicap: A numerical representation of a golfer's playing ability.

Hard pan: Hard, usually bare, ground conditions, with very little or no grass.

Hole-in-one: Hitting the ball from the tee into the hole, using only one stroke.

Home course: The golf course at which a player houses his/her handicap.

Honors: The right to tee off first, based on having the best score on the last hole or being farthest from the hole.

Hook: When a right-handed player strikes the ball such that it curves sharply from right to left.

Hosel: The hollow part of the club-head where the shaft is attached.

Hot: A shot that goes faster or farther than intended.

Knock down: A type of shot designed to have a very low trajectory, usually hit to combat strong winds.

Lag putt: A long putt struck such that the player leaves the ball close to the hole.

Lie: The position or location of the golf ball while in play.

Lip: The edge of the hole. If your ball hits the lip but doesn't go in the hole, then you have "lipped out."

Loft: The degree or angle of the face of the club.

Loose impediments: Natural objects that are not growing or solidly embedded in the ground. Examples include leaves, rocks, twigs and even animal droppings.

Match play: A format of golf in which the goal is to win individual holes rather than tallying the total of all the strokes.

Modified scramble: Also known as a shamble or Texas scramble, a golf format in which the players select the best shot off the tee, move all balls to that spot, and play individual stroke play for the rest of the hole.

Movable obstruction: Anything artificial on the golf course that can be moved without unreasonable effort. Examples include a rake, a pencil, a candy wrapper, water bottle or a golf tee. A tee marker on the teeing area is NOT a movable obstruction.

Mulligan: In casual play only, a "do-over" shot made to replace a poorly hit shot, taken without counting the stroke toward the score.

Nassau: A very common betting game in golf that encompasses three bets: the best match play score on the front nine (holes 1-9), the back nine (holes 10-18) and the entire 18 holes.

Net score: A golfer's gross score less his/her handicap.

Nineteenth (19ᵗʰ) hole: A golf course's restaurant or lounge.

Ninety-degree cart rule: A method by which a golfer drives his/her cart along the cart path until the cart has reached a point where a 90-degree turn would cause the cart to drive laterally across the fairway directly to the ball. The player drives directly back to the cart path after playing his/her shot.

OB: Out of bounds.

Out of bounds: The area outside the course where play is not allowed, most often marked by white stakes.

Pace of play: The length of time it takes to complete a golf stroke, a hole or a round of golf.

Par: The number of strokes that a skilled golfer is expected to make on a hole.

Pin: The flagstick standing inside the cup on the green. Also known as "the stick."

Pick up (PU): The golf ball is picked up prior to the player completing the hole.

Pitching: A high-trajectory golf shot made near the green, intended to land softly with a minimum amount of roll.

Playing through: What takes place when one group of golfers passes through another group of slower playing golfers, ending up ahead of the slower group.

Poley: A putt made that is longer than the length of the flagstick. A player that hits the ball into the hole from off the green has made a "double poley," worth two points vs. the standard one point when betting.

Provisional ball: A second ball that is played in the event that the first ball is or may be lost or out of bounds. If the first ball is found and is playable, the provisional ball is picked up. If the first ball isn't playable (if it's lost or out of bounds), the provisional ball is played and penalty strokes apply. Hitting the provisional ball when in doubt about whether a shot went out of bounds often speeds up the pace of play.

Pull/push cart: A device on wheels that carries a golf bag, used by golfers who prefer to walk but don't wish to carry their golf bags. It is also referred to as a "trolley," especially outside of North America.

Punching the greens: Aerating the greens by pulling small plugs (1/4" - 3/4" diameter) or using pokers with small tines that leave the appearance of a pattern of "punched" holes in the turf.

Pure: A well-struck shot, often used as a verb. "She pured her shot!"

Putting: The golf stroke used to roll the ball on the green.

Ranger: The golf course staff member who provides player assistance on the golf course and who is responsible for keeping the overall pace of play.

Rating: The measure of a golf course's difficulty for expert golfers. The higher the rating, the more difficult the course for a skilled golfer. A course rating number is typically close to the par for the golf course.

Ready golf: Players hit when ready in order to speed up or maintain pace of play.

Rickshaw: A pull cart with two large tires.

Rough: The long grass bordering the fairway. On some courses, there is a "first cut" of shorter rough and a "second cut" of heavier, longer rough.

Sand bunker: A bunker filled with sand.

Sand trap: Slang for "sand bunker." "Trap" is not defined in the "Rules of Golf."

Sandy: Hitting the ball out of a sand bunker and hitting (usually putting) the ball into the cup on the very next shot.

Scramble: Probably the most popular format for charity golf tournament play. Each player in the foursome hits, then the group selects the best shot. Each player hits from that spot and the process continues until the ball is holed out.

Shamble: Also known as a modified scramble or Texas scramble, a golf format in which the players select the best shot off the tee, move all balls to that spot, and play individual stroke play for the rest of the hole.

Shank: Be aware, this is a word you should *not* use on the golf course — it's considered bad luck and is therefore a breach of etiquette. However, you should still know what it is: a very poor shot that hits the hosel of the clubhead and "squirts" errantly off to the side. It's sometimes called a "lateral."

Shotgun start: When golfers are sent to different holes so that play begins for everyone at the same time.

Sit: A term shouted at the ball to encourage it to stick very close to where it lands. This is similar to "bite."

Skins: A popular betting game in which the player who posts the lowest score on a hole among all the players wins a skin.

Skull: A mishit golf stroke in which contact is made above the equator of the ball, resulting in a line-drive trajectory.

Slice: When a right-handed player strikes the ball such that it curves sharply from left to right.

Slope: The measure of a golf course's difficulty for bogey golfers. The higher the slope, the more difficult the course for a bogey golfer. Slope ratings range from 55 to 155 with 113 considered average.

Smoked: A term describing a well-hit long shot, particularly a drive.

Snake: A slang term for a three-putt.

Snowman: A darkly humorous reference to scoring an 8 on a hole.

Solheim Cup: A biennial women's golf tournament in which teams from Europe and the United States compete against each other. It is named after Karsten Solheim (PING).

Stableford: A point system by which you accumulate points based on your score for each hole.

Starter: A golf associate who provides golfers at the first tee with any special information they will need during play and maintains the appropriate amount of time between groups of players starting off the first tee.

Sticks: When referred to in the plural, "sticks" means golf clubs (as opposed to the flagstick). For example, "I'm buying a new set of sticks this season." A putter is sometimes colloquially called a "flat-stick," due to its lack of loft.

Stimpmeter: A device used to measure the speed of the greens. A reading of 5 to 11 is the normal range with 5 being slow and 11 being quick.

Stroke play: A golf format in which the objective is to finish the game using the fewest total shots.

Sucker pin: A slang term for a golf hole situated such that it offers up a risk-reward opportunity when hitting an approach shot to the green.

Sweet spot: The center of the clubface, which will produce the longest shot from a given club.

Swing speed: The speed at which the head of the golf club is moving when it makes contact with the ball.

Tap-in: A very short putt.

Tee box: The area on a golf hole where the ball is first struck, also known as the "teeing ground" and "teeing area." Although you hear "tee box" a lot, "teeing ground," "teeing area" or "tee" are the preferred terms.

Tees: Pieces of golf equipment used to raise the ball on the teeing ground for a player's first stroke on the hole. Usually made of wood, plastic or earth-friendly composite material.

Temporary green: A green used when the permanent green is under repair (common in climates where overseeding occurs) or when the golf club wants to preserve the permanent green.

Tending the flagstick: Standing in close proximity to the hole or holding the flagstick allowing a player to see the hole and then removing it as the ball approaches.

Thin: A shot that strikes near the center of the ball, typically causing a low trajectory. Sometimes also called "skinny."

The tips: The farthest teeing area from the green, usually demarcated by blue, black or gold tee markers. Also called the "championship tees" or the "back tees."

The turn: The halfway point in a round of golf.

Trolley: A device on wheels that carries a golf bag, used by golfers who prefer to walk but don't wish to carry their golf bags. It is also known as a "pull cart" or a "push cart." especially in North America.

Twilight rate: A discounted green fee based on the probability that you will only be able to complete a limited number of holes due to darkness.

Two-putt: Taking two putts on the putting green to hole your ball.

Up and down: Chipping or pitching the ball onto the green and putting it into the hole on the very next shot.

Waggle: Movement of the clubhead, usually back and forth, by a player standing over the ball prior to taking a swing.

Whiff: A golf swing in which the player intends to hit the ball yet completely misses.

Wolf: A four-player betting game that creates a different team on each hole. One player is designated the "wolf" before each hole and decides whether to "hunt" alone for the best score or to pair up with one of his/her playing partners in a (net) best ball format.

Woods: A type of golf club with a round head, usually made of metal or composite materials. The most common woods include the Driver, 3-wood, 5-wood and 7-wood.

Worm burner: A golf shot (not a putt) in which the ball never rises off the ground.

Yips: The inability to make short putts due to nervousness and lack of a smooth putting stroke.

Zone: When you're playing well, you're said to be "in the zone." Sometimes described as "playing lights out."

About The Author

Debbie Waitkus, speaker, author and business/golf networking consultant is the President and Founder of Golf for Cause®. She is passionate about helping others Turn Golf into Gold®, enriching their lives both personally and professionally.

Waitkus, whose professional background includes tenure as president of a successful mortgage banking firm, is also the author of *Get Your Golf On! – Your Guide to Getting in the Game* and a contributing author to the EWGA Foundation book, *Teeing Up for Success*.

As a speaker, she skillfully weaves golf stories into lessons ranging from business and personal development to player development. New, aspiring and hesitant golfers attest that Debbie demystifies golf and rolls out an oversized welcome mat. A seasoned presenter, she has the ability to share information in an upbeat way that resonates well with her audience.

Recognized by the Arizona Golf Association as a Champion of Golf and the YWCA as a Sports Leader, Debbie has collaborated with corporations and not-for-profit organizations in successfully developing and executing charitable giving and outreach plans that have resulted in raising more than $3 million. She considers herself fortunate to have served as co-tournament director, along with LPGA Co-Founder Marilynn Smith, of the Marilynn Smith LPGA Charity Pro Am, providing scholarships for young women to attend college.

Honors and Recognition:

- Arizona Golf Association – Champion of Golf
- National Women's Golf Alliance – Co-Founder
- *Get Your Golf On!* – Author
- Marilynn Smith Scholarship Pro-Am – Tournament Director
- *Teeing Up for Success* – Contributing Author

Honors and Recognition (cont.):

- First Tee of Phoenix – Board of Directors
- Women in the Golf Industry – Treasurer, Past-President
- World Golf Foundation – Women's Task Force
- *Golfweek Magazine* – Panelist
- Arizona State University Sports Business Association – Advisory Board
- YWCA – Sports Leader
- University of Arizona – Entrepreneurial Leadership

Turn Golf Into Gold!®